5-6- ⸮

Dr Muyer - so
special meeting you -
Congratulations on your
leadership efforts -
best wishes
Tom

Living *at the* SUMMIT

A Novel Approach
to an Exceptional Life

DR. TOM HILL
WITH
JOHN & ELIZABETH GARDNER

Goal Coach
Publishing

Lake St. Louis, Missouri

Goal Coach Publishing
1325 Lake St. Louis Boulevard
Lake St. Louis, Missouri 63367

Printed in The United States of America.

Library of Congress Cataloging-in-Publication Data

Living At The Summit: A Novel Approach to an Exceptional Life/Dr. Tom Hill with John & Elizabeth Gardner.

P. cm.
ISBN 0-9667821-3-5 (pbk.)
1. Self-help techniques I. Title
BF637.S4 1999   LCCN
158.1 - dc20   CIP

Cover Design: Baker Advertising & Design/Kathy M. Baker

"When you are inspired by some great

purpose, some extraordinary project,

all your thoughts break their bounds:

your mind transcends limitations, your

consciousness expands in every

direction and you find yourself in a

new, great and wonderful world.

Dormant forces, faculties and talents

become alive, and you discover

yourself to be a greater person by far

than you ever dreamed yourself to be."

--Patanjali

Dedication
Living At The Summit -
Tom Hill

What a pleasure to dedicate a labor of love. This book is first of all, dedicated to Betty, my wife of 18 years, who beginning on May 10, 1980 has been my greatest inspiration and believer. My love for her knows no bounds. Second, this is dedicated to the most incredible blended family anyone could ever hope for. I love each one of them so very much. Finally, this book is dedicated to all those innumerable individuals who are beginning to believe in themselves and want to become the very best they can be. Those individuals who, after years of being on the "treadmill" of life, finally realize there must be a better way, and are looking for the tools to "make it happen."

Dedication

Living At The Summit -
John & Elizabeth Gardner

This book is more than words on a page, it is the realization of a dream the two of us have shared throughout our lives together. It is with great honor that we dedicate this work to our four incredible children. Burt, Wade, Bryant and Peden, each of you have been such a blessing in our lives. We pray the path you choose leads to your own summit of life experience.

Acknowledgements

Living At The Summit -
Tom Hill

In any major endeavor, there are so many individuals that contribute to making the impossible possible that it is difficult to limit my gratitude to a few individuals. With this caveat in place, I want to first thank my entire family, the very best a person could ever hope and pray for, especially my wonderful wife, Betty, and to my daughter Terri and her husband Mickey. They have been my cheerleaders and support team. Secondly, I want to express my sincerest appreciation to Jim Nelson, my primary editor. From the very beginning, he has been there when I needed him with expertise, timely effort and outstanding encouragement. I also want to express my love and appreciation for John and Elizabeth Gardner. They are the best of the best, in every regard. God smiled on me in February, 1997 and introduced them to me while attending a business meeting in Dallas, Texas. I truly am among the blessed on this earth. Also, my deep appreciation to Mary Haviland, who has taken on the task of being the primary person responsible for marketing *Living At The Summit* - bless you Mary. You are one of a kind. I would be totally remiss if I did not acknowledge the wonderful creative support that Katie Baker has provided. Thanks a million Katie - you are very special. In addition to the above, I want everyone to know how great it is to have friends like Becky McDannold, Tammy Fadler, Rodney and Thao Sommerville, Kerry and Sheree Avant, Glenda Williamson, Sandy Cremeens, J.J. Stupp and Kim Pfalz. All have been there when I needed them. Thanks to each one of you. Finally, I want to dedicate this effort to Jim Rohn, Mark Victor Hansen and Brian Tracy, whose writings and teachings have had such a positive impact on my life.

Acknowledgements

Living At The Summit -

John & Elizabeth Gardner

As we all learn through life, there are dream makers and dream breakers — acknowledged here are all of those individuals who are true friends — "The Dream Makers." First to Johnny Etheridge, thank you, we will never come close to expressing our love for you and Pam, as well as our appreciation for your unwavering support of our dream. These last three years will never be forgotten.

To our families – we are truly blessed to have each of you as part of our life. To our "dreamers" at home, our children, the four ultimate gifts from God.

Tom Hill, Dr. Dream Maker himself, our lives will be only one example of your impact. Thank you for being who you are and to you and Betty for living what you represent. Katie and Dick Baker, your friendship with us and your unbelievable commitment to this project are a true expression of who you both are. You serve as an example of what using God's gifts really means. Mary Haviland, a true team player. Your insight, perspective and guidance through this process has been invaluable. You have helped our dream flourish.

We want to express our gratitude to Terri and Mickey Olsen for all you have done, both seen and unseen. Your dedication to *Living At The Summit* is admirable. To our primary editor, Jim Nelson, you have gone above and beyond with effort and creativity — thank you. And finally those friends who have given through work, encouragement and support . . . Kerry & Sheree Avant, Becky McDannold, Rodney & Thao Sommerville, Jay Wood, Hunter Marshall, Tammy Fadler, Sandy Cremeens, J.J. Stupp, Karla Odom, Brandy Seiffert, Tansi Mulligan, Linda Gainey, Glenda Williamson, Frank & Theresa AuCoin, and Scott Chapin.

How thankful we are to have such a tremendous list of those we call friend.

"I could tell you my adventures - beginning from this morning," said Alice a little timidly; *"but it's no use going back to yesterday, because I was a different person then."*

Alice in Wonderland

Foreward
Living At The Summit

Hopefully, *Living At The Summit* will be a faithful reminder for those readers who have started down the path of personal development and for a variety of reasons may have lost their way or perhaps have lost their dream. For those just starting, I want it to be a light - a beacon - a tool they can use on a daily basis. I wrote it primarily as a self-help work, hoping that the novel would carry the message in a more powerful way than in just a how-to book. It is a reflection of my journey and it is intended to be useful - a book that the reader, after finishing, will turn back to time and time again.

> *"At the dawn of a new century, it is the adult life cycle itself—stretching it, taming it, bringing it under control, making it yield its riches—that beckons us all, men and women alike. This is the new human frontier."*
> Gail Sheehy, *New Passages*

Personal growth or personal development is, obviously, very much a process as well as the content. It has been my experience that those individuals who begin the process find it confusing with all the "gurus" and "quick fixes," unfortunately most of which are of more benefit to the writer and their financial situation than it is to the searcher. I have lived and shared this journey with thousands of individuals and know it to be a tried and true method. No living under pyramids, rubbing crystals or magnets over the body and no mumbo-jumbo, just proven, practical ideas that work.

I agree totally with Jim Rohn when he says "work harder on yourself than on your job." Either consciously or unconsciously your success and happiness is a direct result of your personal and professional growth and development. I have been a student of Jim's since 1984 and give him and Mark Victor Hansen an incredible amount of credit for the success and happiness I have been blessed with.

> *"An author should never conceive himself as bringing into existence beauty or wisdom which did not exist before, but simply and solely as trying to embody, in terms of his own arts, some reflection of external beauty and wisdom."*
>
> C. S. Lewis

Personal growth can be successfully achieved working alone, but often being involved with others in the quest is not only very helpful, but also much more enjoyable. To this end, I have created a very unique and comprehensive program for those individuals who are committed to being the very best they can be in all areas of their lives. It is certainly not for everyone, but for those who find a fit, it results in life-changing experiences. One of the foundation concepts is that "who you associate with makes a difference, a huge difference." If the reader has an interest in finding out more about this process, my snail and e-mail addresses are in the back of the book.

> *"What I lack is to be clear in my mind what I am to do, not what I am to know... The thing is to understand myself, to see what God really wished me to do... to find the idea for which I can live and die."*
>
> Soren Kierkegaard

May you soar with the Eagles and find the peace and happiness that you deserve as a beautiful creation of the Master.

Dr. Tom Hill

St. Louis, Missouri
January, 1999

LIVING AT THE SUMMIT

Prelude

Duke Milligan gingerly rescued the can of shaving cream from the steaming water in the bathroom sink. For years he had followed the same routine, heating his shaving cream while he took a long hot shower. Even the exhaust fan and the heat lamp failed to dispel the billowy clouds that hung near the ceiling and fogged the mirror. When Duke opened the bathroom door, cool morning air surged across his hot skin. Wiping the moisture off the mirror, he looked at a handsome but weathered face. As he released the rich warm lather into his strong hand, his mind wandered, as it often did in the early morning, to a distant early morning, when his brother had helped him create a Windsor knot in his first tie. Then the boys had quietly joined their father in the limousine to their mother's funeral.

Duke smiled unconsciously as he thought of his older brother. They had shared a deep lifetime friendship and trust. Big brother had been the smart one, Duke mused, remembering how he was always reading, always asking questions. After their mother died, "Big Bro" had practically raised Duke. Not that Duke really needed much hand-holding, even as a young boy.

As he began shaving, Duke felt a sharp pang of longing for his mother, even though his only memories came from a few treasured pictures and the stories "Big Bro" had repeated. Four decades, Duke thought, and I still wish I had a mother!

Duke did not miss his father, a virtual stranger who had passed through his life like a benevolent distant uncle. Jake Milligan had been a highly conspicuous businessman. In lieu of a relationship with his sons, he had provided the boys with a magnificent estate complete with servants. They attended a fine private school and lacked for nothing — except a father's attention. Jake subscribed to what he liked to call the "Aristocratic British method" of rearing children, summarized in a phrase he found particularly clever: "a father's parental responsibilities begin — and end — with procreation." He mentally patted himself on the back for contributing exemplary financial support. But truth be told, he'd rather have given the boys up for adoption as soon as Anna died.

Anna, his wife, had adored their two sons, who were supposed to occupy her time while Jake conquered new worlds and made ever greater fortunes. When Anna had died suddenly of hepatitis, he had no idea of what to do with the inconvenience posed by his offspring. But he was certain money could solve all problems, another of his favorite aphorisms. So he spent plenty of money and, sure enough, his boys had grown up — quite satisfactorily, he would hasten to add — in his absence.

After his father's death, Duke had insisted that Jake had not influenced the boys in any significant way. But gradually Duke realized that their father's absence had affected both of them profoundly. Why was he so interested in helping others to balance their priorities? Why had Duke chosen the life of a corporate executive? And, more importantly, why had his marriage failed?

Abruptly, he shut out the past. Duke was preparing for a more pressing concern.

1
Chapter

The Board Room

Penthouse suite of IMM, Downtown San Francisco

H eavy burgundy leather chairs slid silently on the thick gray wool carpet; rich leather briefcases snapped open; nervous eyes glanced at Rolex watches and fingered ebony Mont Blanc pens. Tension filled the board room. Mr. J came in late, as usual, with his customary foul cigar streaming pale blue toxins. His ample face was flushed, everyone knew, from several bouts of Baccardi and Coke.

Fresh Armani suits and smooth silk shirts eagerly absorbed the essences of creosote and sulfur. Mr. J bought his cigars in bundles of 25, wrapped in cellophane. The black sticks stuck together like pieces of warm licorice. He seemed to enjoy the ritual of peeling off each cigar from the sticky mass, biting off the end and spitting it in the general direction of the nearest waste bin. No one dared to glance at the discreet sign: "IMM thanks you for not smoking." Only Patricia showed obvious displeasure. After every board meeting, she showered in the women's locker room and changed into a fresh outfit, sending her morning's ensemble to the dry cleaners.

Mr. J took his place as an uncomfortable attendant whisked a cobalt blue glass ash tray in front of the cigar smoker and then disappeared nervously. Most of the board members stared at the glistening, century-old patina on the 25-foot long teakwood conference table. Pat Murphy stared out the window at the Oakland Bay Bridge bathed in fog and rain. His face showed concern for the man at the head of the table, his best friend, Duke Milligan.

At the other end of the table, Mr. J stared at his longtime adversary and smiled. It was a slow, cold, bitter smile through tobacco-stained teeth. Duke returned the stare, unintimidated. In fact, Duke was the only person in the room who seemed relaxed, even amused at the unfolding drama. Through the years, opponents had learned the folly of underestimating the competence and determination that hid behind those sparkling blue eyes and charming smile. Suddenly Duke thought of a cartoon character, the fat mean canine adversary of Goofy. Wasn't his name Pete? And didn't he smoke a cigar?

Duke smiled at the analogy, his blue eyes filled with mischief. Even with his career on the line, he remained calm and confident. He knew he could count on Patricia, Mark and of course Pat. And he probably could convince Bill Mangle to give him one more chance. That was four votes . . . well, three for sure. He needed five votes or the El Frando plant would be history — not to mention his career with IMM.

The other board members sometimes asked each other why Mr. J seemed to hate Duke. Jealousy of his good looks and athletic build? Some offense never forgotten? But then, Mr. J (short

4

for Jongeel) didn't seem to like anyone. He certainly had no friends in the board room.

Duke looked at the eight men and one woman who comprised the board of directors. He considered eight of them friends. They had been to his home for barbecues. They had sailed together under the Golden Gate Bridge and on to Big Sur for a company retreat. They had all dedicated long days and plenty of weekends at the office together. But time was running out on El Frando. The costs were alarming and Duke kept asking for more. Each quarter, the reports were the same. Huge potential. We just need more time. And more money — lots more. Duke looked for encouraging faces, but most stared at the table top and fiddled with their pens. This wasn't going to be easy.

He stood up and removed his suit coat. The knights of old wore armor. Duke wore the board room equivalent of chain mail: crisp blue button-down shirt, gold cuff links, burgundy silk tie and his signature silver gray suspenders. Despite air conditioning, the room was warm; the layer of gray-blue smoke undulating on the ceiling seemed to be closing in. "Let's get on with it, Duke," barked Mr. J, biting down on the black cheroot. The gauntlet had been thrown.

Chapter

2

The Challenge

A t 55, Duke had fought many corporate battles and won
most of them. He knew the power of silence and was
in no hurry. He noticed that one more face looked up
from the table and made eye contact — a good sign, he specu-
lated. Then his own countenance transformed in some subtle
way. He looked . . . resolved, confident. He briefly breathed in
a memory of those glorious college days. Time running out.
Down six points with 80 yards to go. The roar of the crowd fading to a hush. The huddle. Duke's infectious smile as he
quipped, "Time to have a little fun, boys." More come-from-
behind victories than any quarterback in conference history.

A couple of the board members later swore that Duke had actually grown taller. He looked at each person in turn, assessing

what might lie behind the blank faces. Then he spoke softly, "I want one more chance." Duke let the words hang in the air. He was in no hurry and used the awkward silence for dramatic effect.

Then he continued, "I have a plan. It's going to be expensive. It's like daring to drill one more well after 20 dry holes. I'm asking you not to abandon the El Frando plant. Give me one last creative approach. I need six months. We all know the rewards can be huge — potentially the greatest mining success in history. Beyond the copper in Butte or the gold in Virginia City. 180 days. We either strike it rich beyond our imaginations or I leave the company and distribute my stock options to the board. That's all I have to say."

Duke turned abruptly and walked from the room, suit coat over his shoulder. No one saw the smile on his face. He was imagining one of his wild plays — a double reverse flea flicker to his wide receiver streaking down the sideline.

Duke Milligan, CEO of International Mining and Metallurgy, had issued the challenge. But instead of jousting or sword play or gridiron heroics, his future was in the hands of eight men and one woman in a stuffy board room. He walked into the corporate pub and helped himself to a shot of The Balvenie. These should be my best days, he thought ruefully. I drive a Mercedes. I run plants all over the world. We're profitable. But I'm obsessed with our El Frando operation in Cortiza. If the board turns me down, I'll cash in my stock options and be a millionaire. Why am I risking everything on one lousy mosquito-infested piece of jungle?

Duke sipped the strong, smoky single malt scotch and smiled. There was something rooted deep in his nature that refused to dwell on anything negative. He wanted El Frando because he loved the challenge and thrilled at the potential. He swirled the pale amber scotch in the crystal snifter and waited, his mind wandering to South America.

Cortiza. What a country. The proverbial thorn in Duke's side. Every week it was something else. One day, uniformed militia arrived and pronounced 14 violations of the "new building code." A discreet payment to the captain of the militia took care of the violations, for the time being. Then the mayor insisted that more untrained local workers be hired for skilled positions and for better pay. A modest increase in the workers' pay and a much larger donation to the mayor's discretionary fund solved that problem.

But the local politics were merely an annoyance. To a greater or lesser extent, every major project, whether at home or overseas had its share of governmental interference. What made Cortiza so different was the chaos at the national level. The President and his cronies drove exotic imported cars and lived in heavily fortified mansions. Yet the average adult earned the U.S. equivalent of $100 a month. Forty-five percent of the country's 10 million people were illiterate. Schools had become little more than day care centers. Hospitals were understaffed and poorly equipped. Roads were in such disrepair that nearly half of the 10,000 miles of so-called paved roads were virtually impassable.

Meanwhile, the President's military roamed the streets, armed with automatic weapons, while terrorists armed the civilians. Now the violence was increasing as various guerilla forces built their power from jungle bases. Weapons, it seemed, were one of the few commodities that were not in short supply. Even children were often seen carrying rifles. The President chose to ignore the factions. They may have a few loyal followers and a camp in the jungle, but no one could march against the capital and his loyal, well-disciplined troops.

Then, in the past year, conditions had rapidly grown worse. The President took over thousands of acres of land and forced the native tribes to become the labor force of new coffee and banana plantations. Since they had no legal title to the land, legal resistance was impossible. The new plantations were managed by soldiers with their ever-present weapons. New political parties appeared to protest these measures, but as they gained strength, their leaders were arrested as traitors. Small governmental "death squads" roamed the streets meting out instant "justice," and the government's terrorism began spreading to the countryside where the President began establishing army-run "model villages," a euphemism for forced labor camps.

There were protests from international human rights organizations, but their voices were largely ignored. And in the meantime, the President consolidated his power through political assassinations. It was rumored that the CIA was working with some of the strongest guerrilla leaders, but the President's power seemed to be growing like an ominous cancer. The gross national product was actually increasing, yet most people lived in fear and poverty.

Then there was the rain, 150 inches of it a year at the El Frando plant. Rain that turned roads to mud. Mud that filled the sewers. Mud slides that buried roads that were already impassable. Trucks that sank to their axles in mud and died there until the sun came out and turned the mud to bone-jarring hard clay. It had once taken two portable generators and jack hammers to extricate a truck from its adobe prison.

The employees could handle the mud. They could even handle the anacondas and caimans and panthers that screamed in the night. But the bugs were horrific. Mosquitoes, chiggers, and foot-long centipedes. Nasty little orange "devil spiders;" ants that both stung and bit; flies that drank tears from your eyes. One worker had suffocated to death in a black cloud of gnats. There was a particularly exasperating beetle in Cortiza inordinately fond of chewing through insulation on power lines. And worms: tapeworms, round worms, ring worms, heart worms, lung worms.

Plants were nearly as bad. Vines climbed telephone poles and brought down the lines. Roots cracked even the "impenetrable" 18-inch reinforced concrete runways. One plant the natives called the "gympie bush" burned the skin, the pain lasting for weeks; another smelled like rotting fish. Could they ever control just a few hundred acres of this swarming, hostile fecundity?

For miles the land was dotted with steam vents, mud pots and small geysers. Twice already the road had to be moved to navigate around a new thermal sinkhole. Worse yet, the air was filled with corrosive steam that condensed on everything, destroying ball bearings, rusting machinery and constantly shutting down operations. Finally, they had ordered machinery with stainless steel housings and Teflon-coated wiring.

It was maddening. The El Frando mine had already produced the highest grade tungsten and molybdenum ore in the world. Duke had spikes of calcite crystals more than a foot long and pink calcite clusters six feet across. Museum-quality tourmaline crystals were being discovered every week, and the two onsite geologists had shown him assays of rare precious metals possibly more valuable than the primary ores.

But what good is a mine when equipment fails; when red clay turns liquid and buries the road? When power and water and sewer and telephone services are disrupted for weeks at a time? The tantalizing promise of discovery and enormous profits had kept IMM there for nearly a dozen years. Now time was running out. Duke sipped the scotch and envisioned the football spiraling into the outstretched hands of his receiver.

Chapter 3

The Plan

Duke's reveries were interrupted by Bill Mangle who sat down beside him without asking for an invitation. "O.K. you fool. You've got 30 days to put together a team and six short months to show a profit. You won't have to worry about a budget; you've virtually got a blank check. The vote was five to four. And you'll never guess who broke the tie — your buddy Mr. J."

"I don't get it," said Duke. "Jongeel is the only person in this whole company that I can't stand and I'm sure he hates my guts too. What does he have up his slimy sleeve?"

"Simple," said Mangle. "Your offer was too good to pass up. He's convinced you are going to fail. That means you're out. And he gets a share of your stock options. That was a stupid stunt you pulled. Why risk your stock? If you fail, you lose nearly nine million bucks."

Duke leaned back and locked his fingers behind his head, a boyish grin on his face.

"What's so funny?" Mangle demanded.

"Nobody really thinks I can turn things around in El Frando, Bill. Not even you. And especially not that obnoxious slob Jongeel. But I've got a plan. And it just might work. I've got seven short months. See you later, Bill. I've got work to do."

14

Chapter

4

The El Frando Committee

When Duke returned to the board room, it was empty. Lemon spray had failed to erase the pungent cigar odor, but it helped. Too bad the penthouse windows don't open, thought Duke. He noticed the room had already been cleaned and the table waxed again, as it had been every day for the 25 years Duke had been in the company and probably for half a century before that. He walked purposefully to his office and called Jennie to join him.

Jennie was Duke's administrative assistant. Originally from Guam, she had moved to San Francisco to take some business classes. "Everyone needs a good secretary," her father had insisted. She soon fell in love with the cosmopolitan city; even the bitter cold days of wind and drizzle failed to lure her home after she

15

had gotten her degree. When her proud father came to her graduation, he was stunned at the transformation in his "cute little daughter." She had become a beauty. For eight years she had been with Duke and still insisted on calling him "Mr. Milligan" or "Sir." Her smile and infectious laugh could light up a room. More than once corporate executives had made her offers of employment, but her loyalty was legend. Still, Duke took no chances — Jennie earned a handsome salary.

She sat in her usual chair ready to take notes.

"Jennie, we've got a lot of work to do and not much time. I'm going to need you to work weekends for the next month. I really need your help. Can you do it?"

"Sorry, boss. I'm way too busy," Jennie answered, grinning. It was a ritual they had been through many times before. Duke knew that he could count on Jennie, even though he felt guilty about the demanding days ahead.

"What about Alan?" Alan was Jennie's fiancée eight years running. They lived together. They seemed happy as clams. And Jennie didn't seem to mind their arrangement. Who am I to criticize, thought Duke. Their engagement has lasted longer than my marriage did!

"He won't like it much," Jennie answered honestly. "But I know you've only got seven months to select a special team and get El Frando operational and we're going to do it. Besides, I can use the big bonus I'm sure you have in mind for me!"

"How did you find out so fast about the seven-month deadline? On second thought, I know the rumor mill here operates at warp speed. Thanks, Jennie. And you can count on that bonus. Now let's get to work."

Half an hour later Duke sat at his second meeting. His quickly assembled "El Frando Committee" consisted of himself, Mary

Dawson and Steve Madsen. "This is it — do or die on El Frando. Here is my plan. We've tried every idea in the bag. Now it's time for some bold, dramatic strokes. And we don't have much time. The clock is ticking. The three of us have worked together for a long time. You have both been here long enough to know that the only reason Jongeel voted for this project is to see me fail. I trust you both with my career and appreciate your vote of support, but this is only the beginning. My future is on the line. In the next 30 days I'm going to be asking a lot of you — way too much. It means time away from your families. It means seven days a week and . . ."

"Oh shut up, Duke. You're wasting time. Just tell us what to do." It was Mary, Chief Operations Officer. Tall, gangly, shy Mary — she was just full of surprises. But her determination to frustrate Mr. J's plans was never a surprise to anyone. Mr. J had cast the only dissenting vote when she was hired by IMM. He had been trying ever since, mostly without success, to make her professional life as miserable as possible. Duke, who instinctively hated a bully, quietly made sure that Mary felt secure. And under his protection, she had blossomed into one of IMM's stongest managers.

"Like she said," Steve piped in, grinning from ear to ear, "let's get to work or Old Smoke Stack is going to be spending your retirement money. And with you gone, you can bet he'll find a way to get rid of Mary and me."

"You should refer to the esteemed Mr. J with more respect," Duke responded straightfaced. Then all three burst out laughing.

They quickly got down to business. "Mary," Duke said, "I want you to identify the major areas of expertise we need to turn around the El Frando operation. Steve, we need names for each position Mary identifies — the best and brightest in their field. We don't have time for interviews. Be generous with the corporate checkbook and get them on board."

For the next two hours they worked on Duke's plan. No one bothered to mention the difficulties.

Chapter 5

The Search

M ary found her task to be relatively easy. After consulting with her managers, she had identified needs in technology, finance, personnel, engineering and legal/political. Then Steve took over. His first chore was determining how he could build a team in just a few short weeks that would be capable of turning around a plant under the horrific conditions in Cortiza. Duke Milligan needed this team to pull off the largest coup in the history of IMM and Steve would need to find extraordinary people to complete the task. Access to a personal profile for each candidate would be the key. Team building was one of Steve's specialties, and he had learned the hard way that a personality conflict could kill a deadline. With the help of sophisticated databases and several search firms, he assembled his "best and brightest" list. The daunting task was getting the right team together, and quickly. He picked up the phone and began dialing.

Steve looked at his notes. The first name under financial consultant was Sharon Minton. Like all the candidates, she was brilliant. Her professors had called her aggressive and ambitious, but classmates used harder adjectives, like ruthless. Steve was surprised to learn that she was born and raised in rural Indiana, and then mentally kicked himself for stereotyping. Reading the letters of recommendation, Steve began to picture the distinctive Ms. Minton. The descriptions included the following: little time for friends, MA in financial planning in four years, passionate only about the bottom line.

College professors had stated that although some of her fellow students viewed her as ruthless, she was just "intensely focused." She had quickly moved up the corporate ladder as a workaholic, but many current colleagues said in their recent reviews of Sharon that they enjoyed her forceful opinions, hearty laugh and unpolished natural charm. She had been married, but she cited in her portfolio that her work was her single most important commitment. Steve knew that the project needed her focus and work ethic. His call lasted less than three minutes; he made her an offer she couldn't refuse.

Gary Wilson was the next target, the human resources development specialist. His profile stated that he was in his early 50s and had been married for over 25 years with two children. Steve knew how hard it was to recruit people with young children, and was relieved to find that the Wilsons were empty nesters. Like many human resource specialists, Gary was outgoing and affable. His picture reminded Steve of the tycoon on Monopoly, heavy set and jovial. Gary had a PhD from a Midwestern university and many years as a respected scholar before becoming an independent consultant.

He could hardly be more different from Sharon Minton. His characteristics were listed as carefree and prone to hyperbole.

"Gary is a dreamer who often speaks in sweeping graphic pictures," were the words of one of Gary's previous supervisors. His profile mentioned that he never wore a watch. Steve thought the detail to be curious, but was more concerned with how his carefree nature would mix with the drive of Sharon. After speaking with Gary on the phone, Steve felt reassured of Gary's ability and recruited him skillfully, playing on his sense of adventure.

Kevin Klaus was Steve's choice for engineering. Kevin had a lot of experience, but what made him so valuable was his mastery of so many engineering specialties: electrical, mechanical, hydraulics, structural and even a strong working knowledge of aeronautics. The picture provided to Steve made Kevin look more like a military officer than an engineer: square-jawed and upright of posture. He looked much younger than his 48 years. His gray eyes seemed to miss nothing. It was clear that career was paramount to Kevin. Intelligence and self-mastery were terms used to describe his commitment to himself. His profile also listed three marriages and three sons that no employers had ever met. Kevin was characterized as a master problem solver, yet lacked skill in developing personal relationships. Despite his challenge with his personal life, Kevin had been a part of many successful business teams. Steve's discomfort about Kevin's ability to function as part of Team El Frando had been put to rest.

Again, the recruiting process was relatively easy. The opportunity of running the engineering division for the prestigious IMM was a strong incentive. But the clincher was the complex matrix of engineering challenges. Steve looked over the thick portfolio one last time. He was pleased to have landed such a perfect candidate. He wondered if Kevin's marriage could survive a six-month absence, but closed the folder and forced himself to move on.

Michelle Nigeal joined the team as the "computer geek," officially the Director of Management Information Services. Steve found it encouraging that in a male-dominated field, Michelle had excelled. Her heritage was listed as a second-generation American whose grandparents had immigrated from Nicosia,

Cyprus to Boston at the turn of the century. Alone among the team members, Michelle's file listed no formal education beyond high school. She had received several awards which indicated an almost intuitive mastery of computers, software, programming and functionality. Among her abilities was a rare talent of explaining computer complexities to others. The general information in her personal profile stated that she was in her early 40s, married with two children.

Michelle turned down Steve's first two offers. Steve had nearly given up on Michelle, but got her attention when he promised her a live-in nanny, summer camp for the kids and finally a three-month vacation for the entire family in Alaska. It's a good thing we have a blank check, Steve thought as he added Michelle to the list.

The last person turned out to be the most difficult. Wasn't that always the way? Steve thought. The first four lug nuts loosen just fine, and the fifth one is frozen solid. What made the fifth position so hard to find was the mix of needed qualities. Duke wanted an attorney, specializing in international law, who also had a strong political background. Steve had just about decided to ask Duke to hire two people when he met and interviewed Garrett Johnson.

During their meeting, Steve learned that Garrett had been a representative in his state legislature, while expanding the law practice inherited from his grandfather and father. His international experience was limited, but Steve recognized the qualities he was looking for. Garrett was the classic southern gentleman, courteous, conscientious and charming, who had sowed his wild oats in his early years. But he adored his new wife and she was devoted to him. It was obvious that Garrett had gotten it right.

This time it was the spouse who came to Steve's rescue. She was proud to have her husband selected and nudged Garrett into accepting. "I'll keep the home fires burning," she had told him. "I know it seems like a long time, but I know we can handle six months. Besides, when we are sitting on our rocking chairs in our dotage, I don't want you regretting that great opportunity you let slip through your fingers."

Garrett, who resented his occasional business travel trips, finally acquiesced, although it cost Steve an expensive second honeymoon cruise.

The team was complete.

6
Chapter

Team El Frando

The newly named "El Frando Committee" convened 15 days after Duke had given marching orders. Duke had asked two of his most well respected stock holders and three additional employees to join himself, Steve and Mary to approve the Team El Frando candidates, before the team was presented to the board. He had hoped, almost against hope, that Steve and Mary could put the team together in three weeks, but more likely it would take the full month allotted to them. But 15 days! It was incredible. Steve had paid the price. His eyes were sunken from little sleep. His voice was gravelly and an octave lower than usual. But he stood in front of his friends with pride.

"I've never worked so hard in my life. Nor had so much fun. I think we have assembled the best team in the world. If any group of people can turn El Frando into a winner, this one can. I know this committee has to approve our choices. But with all due respect, we don't have much time. I hope you will trust my judgment and let us move forward. Now if you'll excuse me, I'm going to get some sleep."

The El Frando Committee reviewed each resumé. Mary listened to comments and answered a few questions. The possibility still existed that the board might not approve the candidates. Worse yet, the board might suddenly change its tenuous approval and decide to close the entire El Frando operation. After all, it would eventually have to disclose to shareholders the daring expenditure of tens of millions of dollars. If this plan failed, Duke might not be the only one to find himself out of work. A vote of angry shareholders could oust the entire board. The discussion soon turned to strategy: how would they convince the board to approve the team and to support the plan? Ironically, their strong suit was Mr. J, who was determined to give Duke his opportunity to fail.

Duke, it seemed likely, would be given his blank check and six months. If he failed, Duke would take all the blame — Mr. J would certainly see to that.

The committee approved the candidates and then turned their attention to Mary's chief concern, that a new team of strangers, with their wildly diverse personalities, might find it difficult to work together. It usually takes precious time to build trust and esprit d'corps. The personality mix could spell disaster, but they had done their homework and hoped it would pay off. Little time was left for team-building before the five new members flew to Cortiza. With that sobering thought, Duke stood up to adjourn the meeting. He smiled that irresistible boyish smile and saw each committee member's face mirror a response.

"My dear friends," Duke paused to look each person in the eyes, "I have lived long enough to appreciate friendship and loyalty. We have worked together for a long time. Now our biggest

26

adventure begins. The possibility of success isn't the only potential reward here. In fact, it may prove impossible to master the challenge of the El Frando Project. What really matters is that we have an opportunity to work as a team and to make a commitment to something. We have a goal — a challenge — something really, well, *fun*. Yeah, fun. It's time to stop worrying about what might go wrong. We've crossed our Rubicon.

"I have a little gift for each of you." Duke handed a cobalt blue velvet box to each person at the table. The pin was simple. A deep blue background with white letters "TEF" and a glowing red ruby in the center. 'TEF' simply means 'Team El Frando.' I want each of us to wear this pin for the next six and a half months. It is a symbol of our solidarity, of our friendship, our commitment to this great adventure. When we get tired or frustrated, let's remember that we're supposed to be having fun, and that we are friends. The potential rewards are great. Just thinking of the frown on Mr. J's face is almost worth the risk." Chuckles cascaded into the room. "I'll see you at the board meeting. When Steve wakes up, will someone be sure he gets his pin?"

Chapter 7

Board Room, Round Two

The board meeting started out in slow motion. The secretary read the minutes of the last meeting. Roberts Rules of Order prevailed as motions were seconded, votes recorded and issues assigned to committees. The El Frando Committee members, each wearing a new piece of jewelry, waited calmly and patiently, ignoring the billows of vile cigar smoke from the end of the table. "The next order of business," the secretary announced with practiced neutrality, "is the El Frando Project."

Bill Mangle stood. "Duke," he said, "you can still back out of this. You don't need to risk your career on one project."

"It's O.K., Bill," Duke responded. "I know what I'm doing." Duke spoke quietly and slowly. He praised Steve and Mary for their almost miraculous accomplishments. He outlined the qualities of each of the five new team members. Step by step he outlined the plan that the El Frando Committee had put together, including a profit-sharing proposal for each of the consulting team members, should they succeed. The new team members were not aware of this generous bonus, but Duke insisted it be part of the proposal. Even the most senior board members looked stunned when Duke unrolled the budget. Duke had never been shy about spending corporate money, but this venture was going to strain even the considerable reserves of IMM.

Nevertheless, there was little debate. Mr. J growled that they had already agreed in principle; let Duke sing his swan song. Three board members abstained and insisted that the minutes record their unwillingness to support the project. The only amendment came from Bill Mangle, who convinced a majority of board members to give the team a full six months from the day they arrived at the El Frando plant — it wasn't fair to start the clock until then. By the time the team was assembled, visas approved and travel arrangements made, they might have lost one or two precious weeks. The board had formally approved the project with Bill's amendment, not anticipating the consequences of the apparently innocent act. Then, suddenly, the meeting was over. The El Frando Project had one last desperate chance.

Chapter

8

The Sierra Nevada Mountains

S teve looked refreshed and well-rested as he skillfully maneuvered his Miata through the curves. Mary reveled in the sunshine and the breeze blowing through her hair. It was great to get out of the city, even as beautiful a city as San Francisco. They had left the freeway far behind and with each mile the stress of the past three weeks seemed to slip away. While Steve secretly admired Mary's shapely legs, he openly teased her for her white skin. Mary just laughed, especially since Steve was just as pale. They realized it had been many months since either had been in shorts and enjoying sunshine.

Spring in San Francisco had been dreadful: wind, fog and drizzle interrupted by outright downpours. Duke had posted a small framed quotation from Mark Twain on his door: "The coldest winter I ever spent was a summer in San Francisco." The beaches were closed. Mud slides had closed Highway 1 and dozens of houses had slipped from precarious perches on the steep hillsides. The clear skies and bright sun cheered them both immensely. It was nature's omen of goodwill for the project. Despite the serious consequences of failure, they both felt exhilarated. The challenge had been accepted; it was time to think of the possibilities. The rest of the El Frando members were due to arrive about noon. As usual, Mary insisted on arriving early and making sure everything was ready for the planning meeting.

Steve slowed down and turned left to a smaller road. The last two miles were his favorite — sharp hairpins up the steep hillside. Mary didn't enjoy the steep dropoff and asked Steve to slow down. She was beginning to feel both ill and nervous. Steve shifted to second and took the hill slowly, making conversation to keep Mary's mind off the sheer drops. "You know why Mr. J has lived so long?" he asked.

"Don't tell me it's his purity of heart and clean living," Mary quipped with more than a tinge of bitterness. She truly hated Jongeel and his nasty cigars, involuntarily shuddering as she recalled those awful board meetings.

"Well, heaven won't take him, and hell is afraid he might take over," Steve laughed. It was good to hear Steve laugh, Mary thought. Despite herself, she laughed too. It was so hard for her to enjoy herself like others, she thought. She hated jokes. They always made her feel uncomfortable, obligated to respond. She remembered graduate school, sitting in the student center with a bunch of friends and drinking beer. She couldn't stand the taste of beer now. What had happened to her? And to Steve . . . he used to laugh so heartily. The pressures at IMM had taken their toll.

Suddenly the steep incline was over. The road turned to gravel at the familiar limestone wall. Ahead was the company retreat house, an old Tudor hunting lodge built in the '20s that Bill Mangle had managed to secure at a fraction of its value 20 years ago. The limestone had been shipped all the way from Loveland, Colorado, and the blue slate roof tiles had been imported from Austria. Steve stopped at the arched gateway to admire the open beams, the leaded glass windows and the ornate stone chimneys. "I love this place," Steve said softly.

"What a dump!" Mary laughed. Steve couldn't believe that Mary was actually kidding around. Their eyes met. Steve wasn't sure what messages flashed between them. Respect? Companionship? Camaraderie? Determination? Trust? By the time the car stopped and they got their bags, they were focused on the business ahead of them.

Duke sat in his study with the lights off. From his favorite room high on a hill in Sausalito, he could see the lights of San Francisco, the distinctive profile of the TransAmerica Building, the necklace of lights from the Oakland Bay Bridge and, best of all, the spires of the Golden Gate Bridge. A ferry was coming into port and an occasional yacht slipped silently across the bay. But Duke scarcely noticed. His thoughts were on the members of Team El Frando. Maybe I should go with them, he thought. Then he realized he was still trying to be the quarterback. This time he had to trust strangers to secure the victory.

Mary and Steve clearly understood the challenge that lay ahead. They had to build an efficient team as quickly as possible. One discordant member could destroy the entire group. Mary knew she could explain what was expected, what goals had to be reached. She had the easy part. Steve had the daunting responsibility of building the team into an efficient, effective unit. They had done it before, creating task forces that had accomplished wonders, but never in so short a time and with such challenging obstacles to overcome.

Steve opened the massive door and flipped on the light switch. The entryway chandelier burst into light. Mary began opening curtains and light cascaded through 10-foot tall windows, tiny rainbows dotting the stone floor from the bevelled glass panes. There was a chill in the air, but the huge living room fireplace was ready to light and a crackling fire soon warmed the cherrywood panelled walls. Mary was pleased to find the kitchen stocked just as she had requested. Then she moved to the "war room", which had served the old mansion as a dining room and library.

This was her favorite room. The table seated 18 people in blue leather wing back chairs. Along with the place settings for lunch, she arranged five leather binders with the IMM logo. On each binder she placed a Team El Frando pin. Two walls were filled with leather books behind glass. Mary had often wondered about the previous owner who had sold the house, library included. Thousands of books, beautiful sets with heavy leather spines and letters in gold. History and literature, mostly. Then there were the oversized, red leather bird books, dozens of them with color plates. And botanicals, some with handcolored drawings. She had found nearly 200 books printed in the early 1600s, mostly in Latin. How could someone part with these treasures? Or was he just a wealthy man who paid a bookseller to put beautiful old leather books on the shelves?

The fourth wall was the fireplace surrounded by blue and white Delft tile and a hand carved mahogany mantle. On both sides of the fireplace were built-in cabinets with china, crystal, silverware and linen. Throughout the house, everything had been left — beds and chairs, paintings and tapestries, rugs and antiques. There were even antique toys in a toy chest. The closets and dressers had been emptied of personal effects, but so many lovely things had been left behind. Mary felt a growing compulsion to know more about the home's former owner. But for now, she had other priorities.

In less than an hour, Steve and Mary had everything ready. The living room fire had died to glowing coals. Steve had tested his laptop presentation. Lunch was ready. Ten minutes before noon, the company van pulled into the driveway and let out five passengers.

34

Retreat House Library

M ary and Steve ushered the new team members into the library with little preamble. They had rehearsed this moment and knew exactly what each wanted to accomplish. Mary started, "My name is Mary. I am head of operations for IMM. I've met each of you on the phone and want to welcome you to the retreat house. Unfortunately, we won't be staying here more than one day. After we conclude our meeting, you will have three days to spend with your families or friends before you fly out Monday morning. No one from IMM will accompany you on the trip to Cortiza. You will have to meet the employees of the plant on your own, but Steve and I feel certain that with your experience you won't have any major personnel problems.

"We have an enormous challenge ahead of us and only six months. In that time, we are going to ask a great deal of you. We all know that you are being paid handsomely for your efforts. And frankly, we think you are worth it. You are the very best available in this country. But right now, you are five very capable but independent individuals. Somehow, and very quickly, we want you to become a team. You will be working together seven days a week on the most exciting mining site ever discovered. But the difficulties are enormous. And besides all the intrinsic challenges, we have five unique egos who have to learn to get along together. Without trust and cooperation, without a deep respect for one another, and without a commitment to the task at hand, you are just five very exceptional people who will earn a bunch of money and then go home in six months. And you will fail. We've looked at your resumés. We've generated profiles on each of you. We believe that you can accomplish a near miracle. But you have to become a team — and fast.

"I want you to know that the rewards of success will be great. We have gotten approval for each of you to share generously in potentially enormous profits. If you fail, you will still have a very nice nest egg in the bank. But our CEO, Duke Milligan, will be fired, and his lifetime shares in IMM will be lost. He believes in this project and we believe this team can make the El Frando Project a success."

As Mary outlined the details of the profit-sharing plan, the team members' faces registered everything from shock to visible excitement. Each person realized that this mission could change their lives. They had fallen into a once-in-a-lifetime adventure. The Goddess of Fortune was smiling on them. But none could foresee the profound life challenges that lay ahead.

Mary wished she could read each mind. Some, she felt certain, were mentally investing or spending their future resources. Others might be thinking about their families, or the experiences they would be missing in the next six months. Certainly their thoughts were probing the uncertain future of El Frando. Both she and Steve had studied each resumé in detail. They had acquired confidential information that went back to childhood. Mary even knew that Michelle's smallpox vaccination was on her hip and that Gary had broken a front tooth in the fifth grade. Still, there were so many unknowns. What if someone dropped out? What if the five just couldn't work together? Mary sent up a quick "arrow prayer" and forged ahead.

"There is one more thing," Mary continued. "Shots. Each one of you has to have them. You are going into the tropics, and you will need to be protected from some nasty microbes. Typhoid is a snap — you can take pills. Same with your polio booster. You will all have to have a tetanus/diphtheria booster since you have passed the ten-year limit. And there are four more: hepatitis A, yellow fever, malaria and a nice little tongue-twister called meningococcal meningitis."

The group groaned. Sharon appeared horrified. But Mary continued, "A medical team will be here tomorrow for a consultation and your immunizations. Expect the session to take about an hour. I'm sorry, some of you are going to be a bit sore and maybe feel a little sick for a couple of days, but it's a necessary evil. There is some good news. You don't need cholera shots, and because you are getting hepatitis A vaccine, you won't need gamma globulin."

"I hate to ask," Sharon said, her voice betraying her anxiety, "but where do we get our shots?"

"Both arms and both buttocks," Mary responded. "I suggest you take a good long walk afterwards — exercise seems to help reduce the discomfort. We'll give you something to help you get a good night's sleep. Now, how about lunch?"

For the next half hour, everyone ate sandwiches and fresh fruit while each team member gave a short introduction. Nothing personal was shared, Mary noted, but at least they discussed their respective areas of expertise. As expected, the conversation gravitated toward discussion of injections and each had a "war story" to share. After lunch Mary asked each one to put on their El Frando Project pins as a first step in working and thinking as a team. Next came a briefing on Cortiza: its people, climate, politics, the utter upcoming culture shock. They would soon depart in the company jet to the capital, then continue by rail to the El Frando plant. Accommodations were comfortable if a bit Spartan. After a few questions, Steve took over the meeting.

Steve knew his task was daunting. It often took years to build an efficient, unified team of professionals. He only had a few days before this team would be living together in a jungle, working seven days a week, isolated from friends and family except by radio and telephones — when they worked. Challenges could bring people together, or . . . Steve didn't want to dwell on the alternatives. "We all know why we are here," Steve began slowly. "There is no question as to your abilities. Simply stated, you are the very best at what you do. We are facing difficult challenges, but you were chosen because each one of you seems to thrive when challenged. Frankly, I think there is only one obstacle that can sabotage this mission, a totally intangible one. It is a matter of character. No, it's even simpler than that. If you can't get along with each other, this mission is doomed.

"I'm not asking you to become friends, although it might be easier if you were. I'm asking you to be totally committed to your work and to cooperating with each member of this team. Some of you have egos as big as the World Trade Center. Most of you have been successful because of your incredible ability to focus on your personal goals. Now you have to learn to become a team, to use your considerable talents together. Our biggest challenge is not El Frando. It is in this room. If we can't work together, we might just as well quit right now and go back home. Monday morning you fly to Cortiza. In the next precious hours, I want you to get to know each other. Decide how deep your commitment is to a team effort. I'm prepared to give each one of you a generous check, right now, if you decide to quit. But if you stay, you need to begin to build camaraderie. As a company we can't make you share your personal experiences, but each one of you know what a powerful positive effect it could have on this project."

That night, after dinner, they sat around the crackling fire, talking softly. Several were commiserating on tomorrow's shots. Steve and Mary watched the dynamics of the group with practiced eyes. They noted genuine excitement and growing determination among the group.

Mary and Steve left for a moment and returned with a gift-wrapped box for each team member. Steve couldn't help noticing how each person opened their present. Gary tore open his package and tossed the crumpled wrapping on the floor. Sharon carefully teased each piece of tape loose and folded the paper neatly to be used again. But each face beamed as the shirts were held up: dark blue pilot-style shirts with epaulets and zippered pockets. "Team El Frando" was stitched in red above the left pocket and on the left shoulder was the IMM logo. Above the right pocket was the person's name embroidered in white and on the collar of each shirt was a simple pin with the letters "TEF." Steve knew the "team uniform" idea might be a bit corny, but he was pleased with the initial reactions.

Later that night, as each member retired to their respective rooms, Garrett asked Sharon to stay for a few minutes. "Sharon, we leave on Monday for six months, and I need your help. I realize that we just met and this may be inappropriate, but I don't have any other choice. One of my business partners has given me an investment proposal that I have to evaluate before I leave. I have made a lot of money in my life, Sharon, but holding on to it has not been one of my strengths. IMM says that you are one of the best, and I have lost enough money in this type of situation to know I need help. Would you be willing to look over the proposal and let me know what you would do? My financial reserves are very limited; I can't afford to lose money, but I can't afford to miss a great opportunity either."

"Is that why you took this assignment?" Sharon asked. "For the money?"

Garrett looked at Sharon amazed at the possibility of any other reason. "Sharon, right now I have everything I want in life, except financial freedom. My need for money affects every decision I make. I know I need to get out of the trap I've created for myself, and this proposal looks very promising. Then if we can pull off this El Frando Project, my finances will be much better. So will you look over the proposal?"

"You'll have my evaluation by tomorrow morning," Sharon replied.

With that, Garrett handed over the proposal and they both headed to their rooms. As Sharon lay in her bed reviewing the spreadsheets and projections, all she could think of was one thing Garrett had said: "I have everything I want in life, except financial freedom."

The only thing Garrett is missing is the only thing I have, Sharon mused. She tried to imagine what it might be like if she had everything she wanted. She soon realized that she didn't really know *what* she wanted. She returned to her homework, frustrated.

The next morning, Steve felt a surge of confidence as each new team member showed up in their new team shirt.

Sharon returned the financial proposal to Garrett with a note saying "It's a sure bet." The two exchanged smiles.

Mary told the team that after their shots, they would be taken back to San Jose where they would have the weekend to prepare. The game was afoot.

Chapter 10

The Flight to Cortiza

Three days later

Monday morning. San Jose International Airport was bathed in a gentle mist. The smell of sawdust lingered in the air in what seemed to be a perpetual ritual of remodeling. But the team sat together with a warmth of camaraderie. Garrett and Sharon sat next to each other, expressing their budding friendship. Even surviving the ordeal of inoculations seemed to help bond the group. Fortunately, no one had suffered more than moderate tenderness. The unspoken feelings within the team were discernible in their body language — tension, excitement, fear of the unknown, but above all, a heightened sense of anticipation. Sitting together in the lobby of IMM's flight department wearing their team shirts, the team exuded an air of confidence that exceeded any individual's. Certainly every person recognized that this was an incredible opportunity. But the team had already come to the firm conviction that they could, and would, turn the plant into a profitable operation.

As everyone took their seats, the Captain closed the door, gave everyone a safety briefing then climbed up front. Eight luxurious glove leather seats filled the main cabin of the IMM corporate jet. The first two seats were taken by Gary and Michelle; facing them were Garrett and Kevin. Garrett had asked Sharon if she would like to sit with him, but she had declined his offer, stating "I need some think time before Cortiza." She selected the seat at the far back right. The adventure had begun. Recent days had sped by quickly. Now they had several hours to relax and get to know each other better. While a flight attendant prepared refreshments, Gary asked Michelle what her family thought about her coming on the project.

"My husband and my children are both excited and a little sad. I work a lot, so they are accustomed to my being gone some, but never for six months. I decided to come because it was a change of pace, not to mention the potential rewards. What about you?"

Gary responded, "I really feel good about this adventure. I'm sure it will change my life somehow. My kids are grown, and my wife has a lot of other interests. They all supported my coming. The only thing that concerned my wife was that a few years ago I had a mild heart attack that terrified us both. She was a little concerned about me being in the jungle with uncertain medical facilities, but I assured her I would be fine. I couldn't pass up this adventure."

"How is your heart now?" Michelle inquired.

"O.K., but I haven't lost the weight my doctor told me to. I've tried every diet plan in the book, but I always quit. Who knows, maybe the food will be so bad in Cortiza, I'll lose weight despite myself!"

Michelle turned to Kevin. "Is something the matter? You've been awfully quiet."

"Well, no offense to anyone, but I've been sitting back listening to both of you talk about your families and I'm not even sure I will *have* a family when I get home. You both seem to have successful marriages, but this is my third. It was already bumpy with me at home, so who knows what will happen while I'm gone? As exciting as this whole adventure promises to be, it is still just another job. And maybe just another marriage. I guess that's just life."

"That's awfully pessimistic, Kevin," Michelle piped up. "I think you should be excited about this opportunity and about returning to your wife."

"Pollyanna hogwash," was Kevin's reply.

Michelle thought it sounded a lot like "Bah, humbug!" She smiled at the thought of Kevin playing Scrooge. Then she nearly burst into laughter at the quaint phrase, "Pollyanna hogwash." Realizing that laughing might make her appear cold and unfeeling, she composed herself and responded, "Well, my life and family are great. In fact, I don't have any time to do the things I want to do — I bet I haven't even read a book in over five years. But after I accomplish all of my business goals, I'm sure I'll get caught up."

Garrett offered no response to the pendulum of conversation developing between Michelle and Kevin. He found himself distracted by Sharon's solitude. They had been in the air for nearly an hour. The entire flight Sharon had rested quietly in the rear of the jet, staring blankly out the small oval window adjacent to her seat. Garrett stood and slowly moved to the seat next to Sharon.

"That is some pretty intense 'think time' you've been having," Garrett began. "This is supposed to be an exciting adventure, but you look unhappy."

"Confused," Sharon responded, still staring out her window.

"About what?" Garrett said, "if you don't mind my asking."

"Life."

"What about life?"

"Oh nothing," Sharon responded evasively.

"Listen Sharon, I know we don't know each other that well, but you were a great help to me the other day, and if I can help you now, I'd like to return the favor. You said you were confused. Do you mean about why you came?"

"No, I'm just confused about everything."

"You certainly don't seem that way to me."

Garrett seemed puzzled. Sharon was one of the top financial analysts in the country. She was intelligent, beautiful and seemed self-assured and confident. Why was she so despondent? They both sat in silence. Garrett kept his eyes on Sharon, hoping she would realize his genuine concern for her despair. Sharon turned and looked at him with a tear running down her face.

"Garrett, what did you mean the other day when you said you had everything you wanted in life?"

Garrett was surprised at Sharon's vulnerability. Wiping away her tears with his neatly pressed handkerchief, he began, "Sharon, years and years of searching is where that statement comes from. I don't know why you are asking, but I can share with you why I started asking the question in my own life.

"I spent many years trying to please others. I floundered in my early years as a political lobbyist and then as a state representative. But it wasn't until I decided to take full responsibility for my life that I found my passion for law and became an attorney. I got

44

my law degree right after college, but my peers convinced me I could make more money as a lobbyist. Even back then, Sharon, money influenced my decisions. I certainly don't have all of the answers, or know all the how to's, but a good place to start searching might be prayer. It sure worked for me."

"Who do you pray to?" Sharon asked, a little surprised at Garrett's advice.

"Our Creator," Garrett responded simply.

"I'm just not sure prayer is the right thing for me," Sharon replied as she turned back toward the window. Garrett left her alone with her troubled thoughts.

The talk at the front of the plane continued: dreams of what they would do with their money; the excitement of solving the challenges at the plant. Then someone mentioned the shots they had all endured and they laughed. What could be worse than that?

Conversation dwindled as they enjoyed bagels, fresh fruit, orange juice and coffee. Eventually the soft hum of the plane's engines lulled most into sleep. Suddenly Michelle awoke with a jolt. Some vague premonition swept over her. She wasn't certain whether it was a concern about El Frando, her children, or just the tension and lack of sleep? I'll call home to check on things when we get to the plant, she thought.

Chapter 11

Cortiza

Gradually others began to awaken as well. The jet was descending. For a moment the jet bounced through a thick layer of clouds. Then suddenly a lush green expanse burst into view. Moments later they were touching down at Cortiza International Airport. The "International Airport" consisted of a single 4,800-foot tarmac runway carved out of the jungle, two corrugated steel hangars covered with rust and a small stucco building that served as the terminal. "Welcome to Cortiza," Kevin called out cheerfully. He couldn't help smiling at the dejected faces of his fellow Team El Frando members.

The pilot and co-pilot quickly unloaded the luggage on the tarmac as a blast of heavy tropical heat engulfed them. Despite the briefings, none was prepared for the intensity of the hot, humid air. They felt as if a warm, wet velvet blanket had descended on them. Even breathing seemed difficult. All carried their heavy bags to the terminal, gulping the syrupy air. The pungent aircraft fumes mixed with a sickly sweet perfume emanating from the jungle. By the time they reached the building, some were beginning to feel ill.

The terminal offered some relief from the roar of the Falcon 50 as it quickly rose into the clouds. But it offered little else. If anything, it was hotter inside. The customs inspection was cursory and passports were stamped. A guard in military fatigues carried an automatic rifle but seemed interested only in his cigarette. Outside waited a single taxi, a Volkswagen bus that had once been red. The five managed to cram themselves inside with their luggage. They were sweaty and uncomfortable, already longing for the sleek, air conditioned jet and its unlimited supply of fresh-squeezed orange juice. The VW exploded to life in a huge puff of blue smoke and rattled off to the train station.

The five watched in shock as the van passed through the countryside. Chickens and pigs scurried out of the way. Naked children chased alongside, holding out their hands. Older children seemed dressed in rags. None had shoes. All but Garrett were unprepared for the stark poverty. Lopez, the driver, understood some of their conversation and said, "Unrest is increasing every day. Our President for Life is raping our country. Something must be done soon. The soldiers take our food." His voice choked and he grew silent.

"The U.S. can't just sit back and let this happen," Michelle said bitterly. "Senator Ryder is going to hear about this."

Before anyone had the chance to find out how Michelle knew a Senator, Lopez said, "Maybe Guervno can do something."

"Who is Guervno?" asked Gary.

"He is a jungle leader who is for the people — little people like me. He wants America to help him, but nothing ever happens," blurted Lopez passionately. "I could be shot for talking to you," Lopez said, "but I can see you have feelings for the people. We are suffering. We must do something. We hope for Guervno and for help from America."

Suddenly the decrepit van jerked to a stop, backfiring before the engine stopped. They had arrived at the train station. The five struggled out of the van and Michelle promised Lopez that she would help, somehow, then handed him some money. Lopez looked around furtively and stuffed it in his pocket. After helping unload the bags, he started the derelict and drove off in a cloud of exhaust.

The Train Depot

T he prominent train station had once been a showpiece. Now the stucco walls smelled of urine and most of the small mosaic tiles were missing. Dozens of haggard citizens encircled the newcomers, begging for food or money or cigarettes. Then armed guards appeared and the crowd scurried away. Inside, the floor was sticky and the five decided not to try sitting on the oak benches. Kevin returned from the restroom with firm advice about avoiding the place if at all possible. Sharon sat down on her bag and looked ready to cry.

"Look, guys," said Gary, "we are going to laugh about this in a few hours when we get to our cozy little cabins at El Frando. The train will be here soon and we can all have something to drink. We are hot and tired and sweaty. But soon we'll be in our little home away from home and can get to work."

Just then a steam whistle blasted. The train had arrived. And what a train! Great billows of black smoke streamed from the stack. "Check this out," called Kevin as he moved to the platform. The rest of the gang just stared in amazement. Several of the cars had dozens of riders on the roof! As they walked along the platform, they noticed that these cars were also packed on the inside with what seemed to be hundreds of standing passengers.

"Has everything been robbed in this country?" cried Sharon. "There are no seats in the cars!"

"Don't worry," growled Garrett, "first class will have seats." Garrett's prediction proved correct. The car was old and dusty, but there were seats and they had the entire car to themselves. They collapsed with signs of relief on their faces and all five broke out laughing simultaneously. As the ancient steam engine began puffing its way out of the station, Kevin, who was quickly becoming the team's voice of doom and gloom, pointed out that the train had no dining car. Then Garrett launched into a lecture on what he would do if he were the "President for Life." Michelle just stared out the window, growing uncomfortable as she recalled her premonition on the plane.

Chapter 13

A Short Train Ride

The train slowly gathered speed and chugged along noisily. All the windows were open and the breeze offered at least minimal relief from the stifling heat and humidity. The sun, now low on the horizon, had finally burned off the dense clouds and the sky glowed metallic blue. A pair of blue and gold macaws drifted on the edge of the jungle, squawking. Kevin was especially enamored with the insects. "Just look up in the air! Dragonflies, butterflies, beetles — there must be hundreds, thousands of species. And look at the swarms of tiny things — gnats or mosquitoes or whatever. I've got to figure out a way to collect some of this stuff and add to my collection."

"You collect bugs?" Michelle exclaimed, shivering at the thought.

"I sure do," Kevin responded, ignoring the tone of disgust in her question.

"Look at that!" Kevin exclaimed. *"Morpho cypris!* Those are worth $20 apiece in the States! There must be a hundred right there!"

Michelle looked out the open window at hundreds of dark brown butterflies drinking at a large open puddle of water. Suddenly they took to the air in a burst of iridescent blue. "I've got to admit," Michelle said, "those bugs at least are beautiful."

"Butterflies," Kevin corrected.

"Whatever," Michelle said.

The train began to climb, laboring around curves. Every once in awhile greasy black smoke entered the windows, reeking of kerosene and sulfur. "What does this train use for fuel?" Michelle asked, turning up her nose.

"These old steam engines burn almost anything," answered Garrett, who seemed to know something about everything. "They burn coal or wood. Some trains in Egypt even used to burn mummies."

"That's gross," commented Sharon, visibly shuddering. No one disagreed.

Suddenly the train slowed to a crawl as it began negotiating a particularly sharp curve, then jerked to a halt. "What now?" protested Kevin. "These people don't have a clue. In fact, this whole sorry excuse for a country . . ."

Kevin suddenly stopped talking as three bearded men with automatic weapons burst in, speaking in broken English. They confronted the five Americans and demanded to see their passports. Garrett thought of standing up and saying, "What's going on here? We are American citizens." It reminded him of some

54

movie. But as he looked at the automatic weapons and the fierce faces, he remained seated like the rest and took out his passport.

The members of Team El Frando sat silently, registering fear on their faces and pondering dark thoughts. What could be happening? What did these men want with them? Were they going to be killed, robbed, or worse? What would happen to their families?

Garrett looked at each team member with a stern face, indicating to each of them to remain quiet.

Now I've risked my life for a stupid project, Kevin thought, and I can't be a good father and husband. That's my life.

"God," Michelle began to pray, "I know I haven't always done what you wanted, but if you save me from this . . ."

Is this when my entire life passes before me? Sharon thought as she sat in the corner staring at an armed gunman.

Then Gary blurted out, "Please . . ." Gary's protest abruptly stopped with a sickening thump as the largest of the three hit Gary in the head with the butt of his gun.

"Shut up . . . and don't move," shouted the militant. Gary slumped to his seat holding his head and moaning. The blood ran through his fingers and began to drip on his pants. The other gunmen raised their weapons to deter any further outburst as the team members looked on in horror. The leader scolded the gunman and instructed the others to quickly check passports. After making sure the five were the only Americans on board, the leader yelled some words in Spanish. Moments later, five more men entered the train and each took a terrified Team El Frando passenger by the arm and forcefully escorted his charge off the train to a waiting ATV.

Sharon was overcome with the events of the day and wept uncontrollably, whimpering "Oh no" over and over until her guard yelled at her and raised his weapon above his head as if to club her. Garrett quickly sized up the situation and quietly, but firmly, insisted that his colleagues remain calm, do exactly as they were told and obey orders instantly. "Whatever you do," he commanded, "don't mouth off. I don't know what's going on, but these guys are well-trained and well-armed."

Michelle thought back to the vague, disturbing dream that had awakened her on the plane. She kept telling herself that this couldn't be happening; it was all some bizarre mistake. It was all so unbelievable, surreal. Kevin tried to think calmly about what could possibly be happening and what the options might be. Then all five heard the train groan to life with loud bursts of steam and smoke. Garrett knew he would never forget the hundreds of frightened faces that stared from the train cars, and the dozens of others huddled on the roofs. He wondered why the train had stopped. Did the guerrillas set up a barricade? Was the train engineer part of a plot to kidnap Americans? Did it matter? The train slowly gathered speed, laboring up the mountainside, until it disappeared, only the black plume of smoke visible above the jungle canopy. As the train's sound was enveloped in the dense jungle, five Americans felt their hopes fade as well.

Chapter

14

Kidnapped!

The five sat in yet one more dirty, crowded vehicle in their short stay in Cortiza. Michelle had taken off her cotton scarf and given it to Gary to help stop the bleeding. He appeared to have suffered no serious injury. It was growing dark and the small windows offered little view. The vehicle bumped slowly along a red clay road, jungle encroaching on both sides. It was impossible to tell how many soldiers were following on foot. Not that it mattered. One soldier with an automatic weapon was more than enough to intimidate the group. The entourage slowly made its way through dense jungle, branches often scraping the sides of the vehicle. The team had been placed together on the back two seats. Each one showed visible signs of fear. The instructions had been simple: keep your mouths shut and nobody will be killed. Again, a swirl of thoughts filled the imaginations of the captives. Will I ever see home again? What do they want with us? If I die here, will anyone miss me?

One of the gunmen in the front seat turned and looked at Gary. "Hey, Fat Boy. Are you trying to be the brave one?"

Gary was overcome with fear, but hatred began to boil up inside. Weight was the one thing Gary had never been able to conquer, and here was yet another tormentor, mocking him. Even as a child, kids had called him "Slobbo" or "Fat Boy" or "Chubs." Gary had often fantasized about killing his tormentors. Or better yet, becoming the perfect male specimen who attracted the girls and intimidated the guys. Here I am bleeding, kidnapped by an unintelligent brute with a gun, and I'm angry at him because he called me fat! Gary thought bitterly. Why is it that with all of my accomplishments, my one challenge can hurt me the worst. I could show these guys a thing or two when it comes to human relations. Yeah, when pigs fly, and he resigned himself to whatever fate lay ahead.

Time passed and the five tried to sit comfortably as they progressed through the seemingly endless jungle. Gary's head wound proved superficial and soon stopped bleeding. Finally they came to a clearing and the vehicle stopped. A cloud of dust settled on the ATV and drifted into the open windows. Gas lanterns illuminated the clearing. Silently, the five climbed out and took in the surroundings. It was a simple compound of eight wooden buildings. The gray structures stood in the shape of a square, each of comparable size and shape with the exception of the one large building on the far end which appeared to serve as a mess hall. Their attention was drawn to the building at the opposite end from the mess hall. A tall, slim man dressed in immaculate military fatigues appeared from within the wooden shack. He had brown slick hair and striking dark eyes. The captors yelled out, raising their weapons in victory, "Guervno, Guervno, victory for Guervno."

15
Chapter

Guervno

Guervno addressed the group in impeccable English: "Welcome to Natino, the home and hope of Cortiza. Please come in and be my honored guests."

So this is the famous Guervno, thought Garrett. The country's savior that the taxi driver talked about. He's just a polished thug who kidnaps "honored guests." Overthrow Batista and you get Castro. Overthrow the President for Life and you've got Guervno. Just one ruthless dictator after another, while the people suffer. And now, I suppose, our host will find some political use for us. Maybe a big ransom to fund his band of guerrillas. At least he is educated — he knows we have value to him. It would be a stupid waste for him to kill us.

Garrett's thoughts were interrupted as the group was ushered into the building and seated on benches on either side of a long wooden table. A canteen was passed around and each drank deeply from the tepid water, despite their suspicion that the water must be swarming with tropical microbes.

Guervno paused for effect, pleased that his audience was subdued. "I do not consider you captives. You are my temporary guests, and my men will treat you as such. You have absolutely nothing to fear. You may have heard of me." At this point, Guervno smiled. Of course they have heard of me, he thought. Everyone has heard of me. I am the hero of this country and will soon be its leader. "I have but one purpose in life — to overthrow our corrupt President who is destroying my people and our beloved country. I have had many discussions with your CIA. But they move too slowly. They will not tell the American people about me. They are bureaucrats who are afraid to act. I have grown impatient. You give me leverage. If you do exactly as you are told, I will soon release you.

"My contact in the CIA has made promises. As soon as he delivers, you will be on your way. My people know that I am gentle and caring. I suffer when my people suffer. I wish no one harm. You Americans know about revolution. You went to war against England for your own freedom. Now you will help us overthrow a corrupt government for my people's freedom. In the meantime, relax and enjoy your time with us. You will share a simple cabin. You will share our food. You must realize that escaping into the jungle is a certain and unpleasant death." Guervno smiled disarmingly at the mention of unpleasant death. "Now my guards will show you to your quarters."

Guervno's words and smile were polite, but utterly devoid of warmth. The team was shaken by the chill of his eyes when he stared at them. The guards directed five silent "honored guests" to their cabin.

Chapter

The Guerilla Guest House

Actually it was better than they had expected. A gas lantern burned brightly on the porch and two kerosene lamps gave enough light inside to show a card table, four wooden chairs and four bunk beds. As each guest surveyed their new quarters, Garrett offered to make a pallet for himself on the floor. There was a canteen with the same tepid water. Outside the cabin was a camp shower under a large wooden tank of water. The toilet was a series of holes in the ground 100 feet behind the cabin. Each hole was marked by a shovel stuck in a mound of freshly dug red clay. Much to everyone's dismay, there was no privacy and no toilet paper — a stack of old newspapers in the corner of the cabin would have to do.

As soon as the five were left alone, Sharon cried out in panic, "What is going to happen to us? They have already hurt Gary.

And this guy Guervno, did you see his eyes? He's cold as a snake. We're going to be killed — or what if he just sends us into the jungle to die!"

Michelle blurted out, "Didn't you hear Guervno? He said we would be here for just a few days. Besides, God will look out for us. We must trust Him to lead the way. There is a lesson in all of this for us to learn and . . ."

"Shut up, Michelle!" Sharon snapped. "I don't want to hear any more about God. If there was a loving God, do you think there would be countries like this, with thousands of innocent people starving to death? Do you think 'God' wants us to be trapped in this stinking cabin in the middle of nowhere? We're screwed and most of us know it. You just need to face it; we're going to die!" Then she burst into tears, sobbing uncontrollably.

Michelle started to put her arm around Sharon's shoulder, but Sharon jerked away roughly. "Oh just leave me alone!" she shouted, and continued to sob.

Garrett sat back listening to Sharon's words, finally under-standing her comment that had ended their conversation on the jet.

"Get a grip," Kevin said forcefully. "There is no use getting emotional. In fact, we need to stay calm and look at our options. Garrett, what do you think?"

Without knowing why, the group had already begun to look to Garrett for leadership. Everyone listened attentively. "Well, first," he began, "Guervno is obviously an educated person and appears to bear no grudge against us or America, so I don't think we have anything to fear about personal harm. The incident with Gary seems to be isolated, not ordered by Guervno. He wants to use us in some way as bargaining chips, but he also must know that his hopes of leading this country depend in some way on help from the States — or at least, in not making enemies with the U.S. I don't know if the CIA is really involved, but I wouldn't doubt it. It's exactly the type of intrigue they live for. Let's make the best of our plight while I attempt some kind of rational dialogue with Guervno, and see what I can negotiate."

As darkness set in, the group began to feel more at ease. Enough time had passed without incident for them to begin to experience less anxiety. They hoped that the perceived safety of their new sanctuary was not lulling them into a false sense of security. After all, except for Gary's minor injury, and the "fat boy" remark, they had been treated reasonably well. The kerosene lights were actually kind of cozy, although the light had attracted a blanket of moths and assorted bugs to every screened window and door. Sharon finally declared that this trip had already taught her a valuable lesson. "I've been a loner all my life. I don't live well with other people. I can't even manage to work with other people. My marriage didn't work, and now look where this 'team effort' has gotten me. I'm not taking any more chances. I thought this was going to be a great opportunity for me and look what happened. As soon as Guervno lets us go, I'm getting the next plane out of here."

Gary sat on the end of his bunk and looked at Sharon, carefully considering if he should respond. "Sharon, have you ever heard the saying 'history repeats itself'? Well I believe it does and I also believe that our life repeats its patterns. You think every time you take a risk, something bad happens. But there must be good patterns too — if we could just figure out what the patterns are and find the keys to change them. I've figured out that one of my patterns is my weight. I'll go on a diet and lose weight, just to gain it all back and then some. I know what my pattern is, but I don't know why, so I can't find the key. I *want* to lose weight so it makes no sense. I'm trapped in a fat body and I can't get out."

"Maybe we're all trapped," said Kevin. "As long as we're all being philosophical, I might as well tell you that I'd trade places with you in a heartbeat, Gary. People care about you, I can tell. You said on the plane that you have been married for 25 years and have two grown boys who love you. This is my third marriage and I know all the signs — it's not going to last. I have three sons who hardly know me and they could care less. People don't like me and to tell the truth, I don't much care for people. Most people I see don't understand me and how I think. I don't have one close friend. I just can't seem to find a meaningful relationship. And I obviously can't find the right wife. The funny thing is, each of my wives has been so different. It's not like the pattern Gary is talking about — marrying the same kind of woman over and over. Still, it's a pattern of failure. I always go for losers — or maybe I'm the loser."

Suddenly a rap on the door interrupted the conversation. It was the guard Guervno had assigned to them. He introduced himself as Ytefas. Like several other guards, he spoke fluent English but with an accent. Garrett made a mental note to ask the guard about the curious fact that so many of Guervno's men spoke English. Ytefas announced politely, "Ladies and Gentlemen. It's time to eat. Please follow me." Despite themselves, the "ladies" smiled at the old-fashioned title.

As they walked to the dining hall, Garret asked Ytefas, "Do you think I can get an audience with Guervno? He seems like a reasonable person."

"Always remember," Ytefas answered cryptically, "looks can be deceiving." He said nothing more.

Chapter 17

Waiting in the Dark

Garrett looked bewildered by these words, but said nothing. What was Ytefas trying to say? That Guervno was ruthless? Unreasonable? Surely no trusted follower of the nation's would-be savior would dare to suggest something negative . . . Garrett made a second mental note to talk to Ytefas as soon as possible.

As they walked slowly to the dining hall, they noticed a guard leading another group away to a cabin on the other side of the compound.

"Are those Americans?" Garrett asked Ytefas, his voice filled with anxiety.

The team realized Garrett was concerned. Ytefas turned his head quickly and caught Garrett's eye, offering no verbal response.

There are more captives, Garrett thought to himself. What is Guervno planning?

The five-member team entered the dining hall and sat down to eat. Despite their fear, they soon felt the urge of hunger and the instinct to survive. The simple meal consisted of some kind of sweet baked yams sprinkled with a little salt. The only drink was warm water. The five ate in virtual silence among a dozen or so guards, who sat at another table, their weapons still slung from their shoulders. Michelle wondered if they slept in their military fatigues with their weapons. Garrett looked for Guervno, but he didn't appear. Ytefas ate with the other guards and then escorted the five back to their quarters. Before Garrett had a chance to say anything, Ytefas departed into the darkness. Outside, lanterns were turned off and the jungle closed in on Team El Frando.

Jungle Warfare

D espite the darkness outside, the jungle was far from asleep. Insects buzzed and chirped and fluttered at the screens. A wild cat of some kind screamed. The damp moisture of the jungle engulfed the cabin. The team shirts had become uncomfortably moist in the jungle heat, but there were no alternatives. The only light remaining was a single lantern that sat on the card table in the corner. Something scuttled across the roof. Kevin was fascinated by the incredible variety of bugs that clung to the screened windows and door. Most of the larger insects were moths, drawn to the light streaming from inside the cabin. But once in awhile a large beetle would land on a screen with a thud, scattering the other insects into a fluttering cloud that soon settled back onto the screen.

Some of the beetles were four inches long with fearsome jaws and long antennae. Kevin wished he could capture them for his collection. Then he saw an awesome moth, at least 10 inches across. He recognized it at once as the "ghost moth," but for the life of him couldn't recall its scientific name. Kevin prided himself on his ability to remember hundreds of names — he loved the sounds of *Chalcasoma caucasis, Argema mittrei* and *Pepsis atrata,* three showy insects that were the pride of his personal collection.

Then he saw it. A huge black spider, moving slowly down the screen of the door. Amazingly, the insects didn't flee in panic. They didn't appear to even see it. The spider jerked occasionally as errant moths brushed against him, but he continued to move toward the ghost moth. Kevin watched, fascinated, as the spider, big as a man's outstretched hand, moved to within an inch of the giant moth. Then with a sudden blur of motion, the spider attacked. The moth fluttered for a helpless moment and then it was over. Kevin could easily see the half-inch fangs moving rhythmically in and out of the moth's fat body. Kevin shivered instinctively and turned away. He didn't tell the others.

"Who were those other people with that guard?" Sharon asked to no one in particular. "Did anyone get a good look at them? Were they Americans?"

"I'm not sure," Garrett responded, "Ytefas seemed to indicate they were, but he didn't confirm it."

Sharon continued, "Is anyone other than me worried about the fact that there are other prisoners?"

Michelle and Gary were sitting beside each other. She reached over and grabbed Gary's hand at the mention of "prisoners." "I can't believe how claustrophobic this cabin feels," Michelle complained, shivering despite the heat. "I hope Guervno lets us go soon — I don't think I can stand much of this."

"I think we all are concerned, but Guervno said he was going to release us." Kevin was trying to make the group feel better, an unexpected change from his usual role as Scrooge.

Sharon was preoccupied with the potential dangers. "What if we're not his 'honored guests?' Then we're just prisoners and this is some prison camp in the middle of this God forsaken jungle. Guervno may want to punish us since our government won't help him!"

Michelle's clinch on Gary's hand began to tighten. The realization that there were other prisoners was beginning to take its toll. Everyone silently wondered who they might be. Troubled minds worried about what fate lay in store for them.

When I Get Home . . .

Inside, the five felt compelled to talk, no one willing to fall asleep. Too many unanswered questions, unspoken fears — everyone longing to go home. Garrett, deciding to turn the group's attention to something positive, asked Michelle what her plans were when they returned to the States.

"I've done a lot right with my life, Garrett. I'm a good mom, I've got a successful career, and a great marriage, but I don't have much time left over for myself. When I get home, I'm going to thank God. Then I'm going to hug my kids and my husband. And finally, I'm going to take time out for me. I've really been thinking that I could be better at every role I play if I had more time to renew myself. Maybe even catch up on all those books I've missed out on. What about you, Garrett?"

"Good question," Garrett replied. "I hate to admit this, but I guess I'm going to work on my finances. I have a good income, but it seems I'm always living on the edge. Money controls me. My bills are always due before the money is there, and every month it just seems to get worse. I've got some investments, but at the rate I'm going, my money will run out long before my life does. And believe me, there are plenty of professionals in the same situation. There are startling statistics about the deplorable financial condition of the typical American family. We are in debt. We haven't prepared for retirement. Nearly half of us don't even have medical insurance. I don't want to live in poverty; but at the rate I'm going, that's exactly what I'm facing."

Each member of the team listened to Garrett's plight. Everyone but Sharon was amazed that Garrett had any challenges at all.

"In fact," said Garrett, "that's the main reason I came on this trip. I thought I could get my financial house in order with a big success at El Frando. And by the way, isn't it interesting that we are all talking about going home? What ever happened to Team El Frando? Granted, we've been through some pretty bizarre stuff and we're all wondering what is going to happen to us, but what if Guervno lets us go in a couple of days. We could still turn around El Frando. It's still something to think about."

Conversation lasted deep into the night. Reluctantly, each braved the 100-foot dash to the outside facilities, followed by unidentified swarms of flying creatures and darting animals underfoot. Kevin diplomatically kept quiet about the rats he noticed by the garbage bin. Michelle screamed on the way back to the cabin when a 10-inch centipede slithered across the path. But finally, reluctantly, everyone dropped into a fitful sleep, dreaming of tarantulas, cockroaches, uniformed guards, prisoners and tiny bugs swimming in lukewarm drinking water.

Chapter 20

Ytefas

They awoke the next morning to a tropical downpour. Ytefas burst in, dripping wet, to announce breakfast. Waiting until the rain subsided to a persistent drizzle, they ran to the building that served as a dining hall. And so began a routine of eating, talking and wondering when they would be released. What had happened to the other prisoners? Had they been released? They certainly didn't seem to be anywhere in the camp. Sharon and Michelle especially, began complaining of the lack of civilized facilities — private showers, a laundry, a hair dryer. It was impossible to look or feel presentable in the constant heat and humidity. They trimmed each other's hair into short cuts with a rusty pair of scissors Ytefas had found for them, and then both burst into tears when they surveyed the damage. The red clay turned to mud with every rainstorm, staining clothes. Then the sun came out and the clay turned to a fine film of dust covering everything.

For awhile, they complained about the starchy vegetables and the stifling heat, but these topics soon became too repetitive to be of interest. In the absence of books or television or even walking very far, they spent the hours getting to know each other. The slow days almost forced them to discuss personal feelings and philosophies. They reflected on what their families must be going through and what they had accomplished in their lifetimes. They debated priorities and how they would change when they got home. Home. That was the one topic that never exhausted itself. It became the single strongest focus of the group as the glamour of El Frando faded.

The five would-be philosophers latched on to the idea that they were all locked into patterns of behavior, and mostly negative patterns at that. It was Garrett who came up with the quote he attributed to Thoreau, that "most men lead lives of quiet desperation." No one disagreed very strongly. Ytefas was a frequent bright spot as one day slowly melted into another. He was articulate and, unlike many of the other guards who seemed surly and aloof, he always seemed upbeat. They gradually developed a certain respect for him. Garrett, especially, spent time talking with him quietly and alone.

21

Chapter

Where in the World is Team El Frando?

San Francisco, Headquarters of IMM

D uke paced restlessly, his brow furrowed with worry. For days Jennie had been calling the El Frando plant. Nothing. The train had arrived at the plant late as usual, but without the expected passengers. No Americans had boarded the train, he had been assured. What could have happened? The flight manifesto showed that all had arrived safely at the airport. They had checked in with customs. Then, nothing. They had not gotten a taxi. They had not rented a car. They had not boarded the train. They had simply vanished.

75

Duke had called his Senator, not exactly an old friend, but one who appreciated Duke's generous campaign contributions. The Senator's office reported the same results — nothing. Team El Frando was missing without a trace. Duke wondered bitterly if somehow Mr. J could be behind this, sabotaging his team in order to assure failure. But Duke doubted if even Mr. J would go that far. Something was very wrong, and Duke felt totally helpless to do anything about it.

Two days after the team's departure, the calls had started coming. With each call, the level of urgency increased. Jennie had tried to be reassuring: "No, there is no problem we are aware of. We will have them call as soon as possible." But as the days passed, Duke sent tickets to each of the families to travel to San Francisco. They gathered in one of the IMM conference rooms and Duke gave them the alarming news. Team El Frando was missing. He would spare no expense to find out what had happened. While family members appreciated Duke's sincere efforts, they returned home heavy hearted, fearing the worst.

Several days later Duke called in his assistant. "I don't know what else to do Jennie," Duke said in a slow, tired voice, "but I am responsible for those people, maybe even responsible for their deaths. One way or another, we will find Team El Frando. You've got my word!"

Jennie knew better than to disagree.

Chapter 22

Reprieve

Finally, 12 days into captivity, Guervno came to the cabin and announced that he had reached an agreement with the CIA. The "honored guests" would be released in the morning. He gave a cursory apology for their inconvenience, turned and left, ignoring questions from Garrett.

"Wow, can you believe it? We're going home!" exclaimed Sharon.

"What do you think, Garrett? Can we trust him?" several voices asked.

"I think so," said Garrett. "Certainly he can bear us no personal ill will. I, for one, am going to sleep well tonight, for the first time since we were captured."

But not everyone shared Garrett's apparent confidence. Michelle was excited but uneasy. Something didn't feel right and she usually trusted her instincts and premonitions, however vague. She couldn't explain her feelings, even to herself, and didn't even try to express her misgivings to the others. Kevin kept thinking of that huge spider and the ghost moth. Something about Guervno reminded Kevin of that spider, moving slowly toward a prey that was oblivious to imminent danger.

They discussed taking the train to El Frando and getting on with their assignments, but the consensus of the group was to return home. In just a few short days, each had taken a hard look at their priorities. Everyone agreed that this had been an unforgettable experience, something to tell the grandchildren. And they admitted with considerable relief that none was really the worse for their days in the jungle. The most serious concern had been the possibility of infection in the cut on Gary's forehead, but it had healed without incident. It was clear that they wanted to go home. Buoyed by such thoughts, each shared what they would do the first day they returned. Take my wife to the nicest restaurant in town. Take my boys fishing. Sell my BMW and buy a Ford Taurus. Start walking five miles every day. Soak in a bubble bath with scented candles burning. Put on crisp, fresh clothes. Drink fresh-squeezed orange juice. Run the air conditioner all day long! Get my hair styled.

All five lay in their simple cabin, thinking of the pleasures of home; yet something felt amiss. Maybe it was the nearby company of armed guerilla warriors. Or the nagging worry that Guervno might not follow through with his promises. Or the constant discomfort of jungle critters, inside and outside the primitive cabin. Soon after everyone had drifted into sleep, Michelle woke to a gentle rap on the door.

Chapter 23

Out of the Frying Pan . . .

M ichelle sat up with a start, wondering what kind of animal was trying to get in. She lay silently, deciding to ignore the sound. The tapping continued — probably Poe's Raven, Michelle thought grimly. Reluctantly, she got up and walked to the door, wishing she had a gun. This is stupid, she thought. Within a hundred feet there are a dozen armed guards; it must be a raccoon or 'possum, or whatever similar animal lives here.

When she reached the door and looked into the darkness, she saw nothing. She nervously whispered, "Who's there?" immediately feeling foolish.

To her surprise, a voice whispered back, "It's me, Ytefas."

Michelle slowly opened the door, not knowing what to expect, and realizing that he could have simply let himself in. He was alone and stepped in quietly.

"Wake everyone," he whispered urgently. Michelle didn't need to be told that something was terribly wrong. She started to light a kerosene lamp, but Ytefas stopped her.

"Please," he said, "let's keep the room dark. I have a very important message to give all of you. I shouldn't be here, but I had to come. Please hurry, and be as quiet as possible."

Chapter

Death Sentence

In a moment, the group was assembled in the middle of the room, hearts pounding anxiously. Ytefas spoke softly: "I don't know how to tell you what I have to say. And I don't know why you should trust me. Guervno is a dedicated man. He will stop at nothing to save his people. He is tough, well-educated and totally committed to overthrowing the President for Life and his corrupt government. He desperately needs help from the U.S. but the CIA has refused to help him. They have even told him that they will turn him over to the President for Life if he does not immediately release you. Guervno is furious. He wants to use you as an example. He is not going to release you. You will be executed at daybreak. Guervno has prepared a press release to his followers that you are five CIA spies, sent to Cortiza to execute him and put an end to the rebel cause. He knows that his power will grow if the people think the Americans are trying to help the President for Life.

"I feel so very sorry for you. Guervno has already told his soldiers of his plan. He will break camp in the morning and move farther into the jungle. It is getting too dangerous here for us. Government troops will be looking for us in the morning and your CIA has told them where we have been camping. But Guervno has many places to hide and even the government troops will not follow us very far into the jungle.

"You will be released in a clearing by a fork in the road and told to follow the road to the railroad tracks where the train will take you back. But on the way, you will be ambushed by his riflemen hiding in the jungle. You will be shot like animals. Guervno wants it to appear that he had nothing to do with your murder. But his people will know, and they will celebrate his heroic cause. He will become an even greater hero, at the expense of innocent victims. You have my deepest sympathy, but there is nothing I can do. Still, I had to give you time to get your souls in order. Please don't try to escape. Death in the jungle is cruel.

"You asked about the other prisoners. They were Canadians. Guervno held them here for six weeks. Three days ago, they tried to escape. They were caught and hanged. Their bodies will be found with yours. No explanation of their death will be offered. At least you will die quickly and without pain. You are doomed. Prepare for your death. If you want to leave messages for your loved ones, here are some pieces of paper. Leave them under a mattress and I will do my best to get them delivered. I promise. But you must write in the dark. I am afraid someone may come. I am sorry. God have mercy on your souls."

25
Chapter

Death Row

With that, Ytefas left as silently as he had come. It was as if the Angel of Death had come to them in a dream, giving them the opportunity to make peace with their Maker, but offering no hope for escape. They must now prepare to cross the River of No Return.

Silence. Even the jungle sounds were subdued. The stunning blow seemed to paralyze the team members. Ytefas's words hung in the air like a sword poised to drop. Then Sharon began to cry softly, followed by Gary. All their hopes and dreams and plans would soon die in a distant jungle.

Even Garrett had no plan. He had spent enough time with Ytefas to believe and trust him. Garrett gathered the others together and quietly led them in fervent prayer. It had been many years since Garrett had prayed with such conviction. He had been traveling so much that he hadn't been to church as much as usual. They began to recite The Lord's Prayer. Soon the five stood in a circle, holding hands, reflecting on their lives, and on their imminent deaths.

"I've always been pretty good at giving comfort to others," said Gary. "At least I've tried to be a good friend and a good listener. Mostly, I just wanted others to like me. Now we only have five hours until daybreak. Maybe a few hours more before we are released in the jungle. Yet I feel a strange kind of power in the midst of the helplessness. Very few people are permitted to know the time of their death. We are prisoners on death row. I'd like to say something comforting to all of you, but I've only got a few hours to accept my own death."

"I can't believe how calm we all are," said Sharon. "You'd think we'd be screaming. Maybe this is all too unreal. We can't really believe it is happening, and yet we know Ytefas was telling us the truth. I don't consider myself an atheist, but my spiritual life has been a void, empty of meaning and understanding. I attended church with my parents as a child, but it was all ritual and form. I felt guilty that I said the prayers and sang the hymns, because they meant nothing. I just didn't connect. So as an adult, I just ignored religion. Now I want to believe in something. I want to believe that there is a God who really cares, or a heaven where we live happily ever after. I know it doesn't make sense, but if I could live my life over, I'd go on a spiritual quest. I'd try to find some meaning in life, besides just being alive. I'd try to find something to hold on to you know, a real anchor, not just a crutch."

For some reason, four faces looked at Kevin at the same time. They expected him to say something. No one was surprised when he spoke in a soft voice. "I've always been intolerant. Even when I was a kid, I'd make fun of adults who made mistakes in grammar. If I didn't know how to make friends, at least I could show them how much smarter I was than they were. Sharon said she never connected with God or religion. Well, I never connected with anything or anyone. I always excelled in school, but never loved anything, not science or math or literature. I just learned it. I never traded baseball cards or played sports. I was the classic loner.

"Maybe that's why I became fascinated by bugs. I could spend hours by myself watching them, collecting them, learning their names. Isn't it interesting that the one thing that attracts me — giant spiders and beetles — repels most people. Garrett talked about being passionate; I don't even know what passion means! Can you have passion if you never share your feelings with others? I can still remember reading John Donne's phrase, 'No man is an island' and thinking: that's exactly what I am — an island.

"I thought I cared about the women I married, but I just dumped my emptiness on them. If by some miracle we get out of this, I'd like to try to change. Maybe I can learn to depend on someone, but I don't know if I can. You are the only people in the world I could call friends and I've only known you for a few days. It's just so hard for me to share my feelings with others that I'm not even sure I have any real feelings to share. I've always been afraid that if I shared my deepest thoughts and feelings, someone would ridicule me, the way I've always ridiculed others. I don't want to feel vulnerable. Except, maybe at this moment, I don't care if I'm vulnerable. I mean, what is the point in holding back feelings when our lives seem to be almost over. Tell you all what. If somebody's God saves us, I'm going to find a way to build some solid relationships, beginning with my long-suffering wife, if she will forgive me. And beginning with any of you who can stand being around me. I mean it. I'm going to find an honest-to-God relationship where I can be honest and caring. Listen to me! I'm beginning to sound like a blubbering therapist."

Kevin stopped, surprised at himself. He knew the unique stress had elicited thoughts and feelings he had never before expressed or even felt. But if "someone's God" really did reach down and pluck them from danger, would any of them really change — or were these just some desperate promises with little substance?

Gary broke the brief silence. "My earliest childhood memory is someone calling me 'Fatso.' I was always the last chosen in gym class. After everyone else was chosen, someone would say, 'Come on, Fat Boy, oink, oink. I guess we have to take you.' Of course I laughed with them as they laughed at me. They didn't sense the pain through my laughter. Or maybe some of them did. But to this day, I've done nothing about my weight. What is wrong with me? It's like I want to be fat and humiliated. I know my weight is slowly killing me. My blood pressure is too high. My heart has already cried out for help. And I know what I have to do: eat sensibly and exercise.

"You know what? I've got a PhD from the University of Illinois. That took a lot of work and dedication. But I'm too weak to stop eating chocolate and ice cream and french fries. Now in a few hours, some jerk is going to say, 'I've got the fat boy!' And my life will be over. I hate the way I've wasted my miserable life. I know it's too late now. I've hated my fat body for nearly half a century without doing anything. It took a heart attack for me to give up smoking, but I still can eat a gallon of ice cream at one sitting. But if that miracle happens and the CIA can get here before morning, I promise — on the lives of my wife and two sons — that I will lose 75 pounds in the next year."

"Isn't it truly mind boggling that we are all looking at our lives and making promises to live differently?" Michelle commented. "We are all intelligent and well-educated. We all earn good money. But we all seem to have screwed up our lives. Now we are filled with regrets and promises to change our lives. Empty promises that come from our desperation. Why didn't we make these promises when we had the power to make them happen? I have a good marriage, but with a little more focus it could be incredible! I have two girls whom I love dearly, but half the time they think I'm a nag and a crab.

"I'm a whiz kid around computers and technology, but spend way too much time in front of a computer screen. I have always felt I had a special relationship with God, but I can go for weeks without prayer or contemplation. I just feel that my life is totally out of balance. I never seem to have time for myself and the time I have with my husband and my kids is always interrupted with my work. I seem to be going faster and faster without getting anywhere — you know, the classic treadmill metaphor, that's me. There has got to be some way of having it all, a balanced life. And that is my wish, no my promise, if we get out of this night-mare.

"I don't know if God is going to intervene and snatch us from the jaws of death, but if He does, well, I think each one of us is going to change, permanently and for the better. All these years I've been deeply religious and yet I couldn't walk the talk. I knew I needed to do better, but until tonight, I didn't fully realize how important it was to set priorities and keep to them. We can make a pact among ourselves, right now, to help each other to change."

"What's the use," muttered Kevin. "We can all measure our future in hours and minutes."

"Shut up," said Garrett with enough conviction that even Kevin was too intimidated to object. "We all know that our future is pretty grim. But it doesn't do any good to give up in despair. Even if these are our last hours, why not try to make them mean-ingful somehow? You all know my financial situation. I really don't want to die. But right now, I'm more worried about my family than even myself. How could I have done this to them? My wife will have to go back to work. My kids will face years of debt after college. What a legacy. And it is all because of my self-ishness. I wanted the best, the fastest, the most expensive of everything — and all at once."

It was now past midnight. The air was heavy with remorse and fear, but the sense of camaraderie was almost tangible. The five had all returned to their beds, yet they continued talking, refusing to sleep away their last few hours on Earth. "Never in a million years would I have dreamed my life would end this way," Sharon observed, echoing the thoughts of her teammates. "Just when I thought I was on my way to the top, I'm headed to face a death squad. It reminds me of the fickle Wheel of Fortune we read about in Renaissance drama class."

Escape!

S uddenly Michelle heard a familiar gentle knocking at the door. This time she hurried to see who it was, and once again it was Ytefas, who moved quickly and silently into the room as the prisoners gathered around expectantly. "My friends," Ytefas whispered, "I cannot let more innocent people die. I have served and supported Guervno. I always felt that he offered hope to our country. But I cannot support the slaughter of innocent people, even in service of a worthy cause. I am willing to risk my life and betray my leader, if you are willing to follow me. I have a plan. I think we can escape, but you must follow me without question or hesitation. And you must decide quickly."

Garrett spoke, hoping he was speaking for everyone. "It seems to me we have two choices: stay here and face certain death, or put our trust in Ytefas. We know the result of the Canadians' attempted escape. Thank you, Ytefas, for your courage. I accept your offer. 'Now is the hour for the dauntless spirit . . . now for the stout heart.' It's from Virgil," Garrett explained to his friends.

The others quickly muttered assent.

"Cover your face and hands with this stuff," Ytefas whispered. "Do not make a sound. One by one, crawl around to the back of the cabin and wait for me. I'm the only one on duty, but I want to make sure that everyone is asleep."

Ytefas left quickly and quietly, leaving the five to get ready. The "stuff" Ytefas handed them was black and waxy. Soon their hands and faces were transformed to ominous black masks. They quickly agreed to leave their few belongings, taking the one flashlight, a box of matches and the two canteens. They regretted that one canteen was only half full, but it was too late to worry about that now. One by one they slipped out the door and crawled to the back of the cabin. A moment later Ytefas appeared and they followed him single-file into the dark, and into another chapter of their lives.

Chapter 27

In the Jungle

As they stumbled through the darkness, Gary remembered his favorite psychology professor, Dr. Gates, who claimed that 80 percent of an adult's character and personality has been established at age eight. Unless, said Gates, you have a "Significant Emotional Experience" (SEE). This, thought Gary, is definitely our SEE!

Sharon couldn't believe the profound depth of the darkness. She, like the others, held her hand in front of herself, keeping physical contact with the next person. You'd think the sky would be bright with stars, she thought, and then remembered the dense cloud cover that had so often closed them in. Even without the clouds, the jungle canopy could turn bright daylight into deep shadows.

They moved slowly and the ground was fairly level, but Gary was soon breathing heavily, gulping for breath. Still, they walked without resting. The trail often branched into two trails and as Ytefas chose the way silently, each wondered if their guide really knew where he was going. They lost track of time in the endless jungle. Most of the time the path was passable, but every few minutes they would have to duck under branches or climb over a mossy log. They brushed into cobwebs and felt wings brush their faces. They were bone-tired and growing numb, moving step after mechanical step.

Gary was so exhausted that he almost didn't care if he stepped on a snake or ran into an ambush. He didn't know if he was stumbling toward death or salvation. He was certain that any moment his heart would explode and the pain would be over. He could lie down and sleep, or die; it just didn't matter.

Then it began to rain. The path grew slippery. They stubbed their toes on gnarled roots. They fell on bruised knees. They cursed the rain, Cortiza, El Frando, God, the Devil, Guervno and the eternity of trudging hour after hour without rest. At times the path seemed to be nothing but a web of exposed roots, slippery and hostile. Then, almost imperceptibly, they realized that the darkness was lifting. They could see! The utter black sky was turning dark gray. Daybreak was coming. Ytefas stopped the group and they immediately sat down, oblivious of the mud. They couldn't get any wetter. "Ohhh, how I hate this rain!" Michelle burst out.

"No, no, lady," Ytefas protested. "The rain has saved us. We have walked through the jungle for many miles. The rain has washed away our footprints. It will be difficult for them to know which trail we have taken. Even hunting dogs could not follow our scent after the rain. We can rest for only an hour. Guervno must realize by now that we are gone."

As the team rested, all they could think of was the possibility of freedom. They might see their families again. How wonderful it would be to go home, with a chance at a new life.

As the hour grew to a close, Ytefas stood and spoke, "We must go."

"Will Guervno find us?" Sharon asked, unsure if she really wanted to know.

"It's not likely. We have been well hidden in the jungle and we only have a few more miles to shelter. We should be safe if all of you can make it just a few hours more." Ytefas continued through the jungle.

The team was glad that most of the trip had been in the dark. Now, not only could they hear the snakes, they could see them slither across the path in front of them. Dozens of snakes, all different sizes and colors, perhaps driven to high ground by the rain. Kevin decided he would begin his study of snakes, if he made it home. Bugs covered the trees, just as they had the screens of the windows of the cabins. Several times, Michelle could have sworn the trees were moving due to the swarming insects. She wished that Kevin hadn't informed her that they were giant cockroaches. Ytefas seemed to ignore the movement of the jungle. He continued to choose each path carefully, reassuring the team of each new direction.

"We will stop for one last short rest," Ytefas said as he noticed the team growing ever more weary.

"I think we are safe now. We have only a little longer to walk, about two kilometers ahead, that is about a mile in American. There is a safe haven there where you can rest for a few hours, or several days if necessary. Even Guervno doesn't know about it, so don't worry. You can talk now. We are going to make it."

Refuge

The five were bruised and exhausted, muddy and dripping wet. Kevin had a nasty deep scratch just above his knee with a trickle of blood that disappeared into his sock. But none of that mattered. The five had made it. They looked at each other and commiserated at the sorry sight of matted, dripping hair and mud-stained clothing. Their faces still wore the black, greasy paint. They looked like miserable ghouls on a rainy Halloween night, and despite themselves, they had to laugh at the incongruous sight. A light drizzle continued, but the sky was bathed in the warm colors of sunrise. They struggled gamely to their feet for the last mile, "American."

Even Gary, who had suffered more than the others, stood without complaining. He had earned considerable respect that day. As

95

they began walking again, his breathing was labored. And he fell more often than the others on the slippery mud. But he kept up, determined to struggle with every ounce of reserves. Twenty minutes later Ytefas held up his hand for the group to stop. "That's it," he said, pointing to a cabin that had just come into view.

"How in the world did you find it, walking through the jungle in the dark and with all those intersecting trails?" Kevin asked.

Ytefas smiled with pride. "Stay here and rest," he advised the group. "I need to check out the cabin and secure the area. I'll wave my hand in a circle over my head when it is safe to come ahead." With that Ytefas walked ahead and briefly disappeared from sight. Soon he reappeared, giving the all-clear signal and they began the last short march to what they hoped was some food and a bed. Garrett led the way and entered the building without knocking, shocked to see a bearded man, middle-aged, dressed in guerilla fatigues!

Henry James

Betrayed! That was Garrett's first thought. But Ytefas smiled and introduced the stranger. "I would like you to meet my esteemed friend, Henry James. A man of great wisdom and knowledge. He is my mentor. I used to follow Guervno, but I gradually realized that if and when Guervno seizes power, one dictator will simply replace another. I have been waiting for my chance to escape. When you five were taken prisoner, and I discovered what Guervno had in store for you, I knew it was time to take the risk. I sent Henry a message to meet me here. I am so glad we have all made it. Now wash up and eat. Then go to sleep. You will be safe here. When you have all rested, we will make plans to get you back to your homes in the United States. You must go home. As long as Guervno is alive, your lives are in danger. You must forget your plans to work at the El Frando plant. I am sorry if this is a disappointment, but at least we will get you home safely. That is enough talk for now. Welcome."

Henry was a man of medium height and build. His handsome, gentle face was enhanced by graying hair and warm silvery blue eyes. Henry had not said a word, but his aura and gentle smile inspired trust. Besides, the five had to trust someone. A large pitcher of hot water sat on a woodburning stove, and each washed in turn. Even in the tropical warmth, the glow of the stove felt good, and their clothes began to dry as they ate cold, sweet rice pudding and thin strips of sweet potatoes, fried and salted. The simple food was relished with gratitude. Moments later, five bedraggled Americans were asleep in their damp clothes. The first to awaken was Michelle, surprised to discover the sun setting; she had slept nearly 14 hours! Her muscles ached and she limped badly on blistered feet.

As she sat on the side of her bed, Henry quietly brought a small tub of warm water filled with brown leaves. He motioned for Michelle to soak her bare feet and she reluctantly complied. The leaves smelled unpleasant, like mildew or wet burlap; she couldn't quite place the odor. For a second, the water stung her tender feet. Then the pain went away and the warmth soothed her aches and bruises. When she took her feet out of the water, she was shocked to find them stained dark brown. But she had to admit they felt much better.

One by one, the others awoke and Henry ministered to each. The scratch on Kevin's leg had already turned an angry red, but the yellow-green poultice Henry held to the wound was as cool as alcohol, and the pain immediately subsided. Everyone ate again, delicious cold rice in some kind of sweet milk, perhaps coconut, and warm bread that looked like brown tortillas but tasted like chestnuts. They all drank a very sweet green tea. It tasted like mint and almonds. No one felt like talking. They just relaxed, dressed in simple robes that had been placed at the foot of their beds. They gratefully let Henry wash their clothes in a kettle of water boiling on the wood stove. It grew dark. Some slept; some dozed; some just rested in a mindless daze. Their emotions had been on overload for so long, that they just needed time to recover. As they fell asleep that night, each wondered vaguely about this strange Henry. Little did they know how profoundly he would influence each one of them.

Chapter 30

R & R

Morning arrived with a welcome stream of sunlight. The five awoke refreshed and well on the way to a full recovery. There was no sign of infection in Kevin's leg. He knew the dangers of even simple wounds in the tropics. His grandfather had been stationed in New Guinea in the Second World War and had returned after losing a leg to gangrene from a deep scratch on a rosebush. "Not a bullet or even shrapnel — just a rosebush with soft pink flowers. It was only a scratch. And it nearly killed me." Kevin had recalled his grandfather's words with dread when he saw his leg beginning to swell. And now there was nothing but an innocent-looking scratch.

The group dressed in their washed clothes, wrinkled, but clean and serviceable. Then Henry served a tasty stew with more of the brown fried bread. After the unusual but welcome breakfast, the questions began tumbling. For the first time, Henry spoke: "I am glad you made it safely to my cabin here in the jungle. Ytefas is a good man, you did well to trust him. I'm an undercover agent working for the CIA as a freelance operative," he explained. "They depend on me for information on what is happening in the camps. Guervno's influence is growing quickly. Many people think he will soon be able to overthrow the President for Life. But I assure you, Guervno will be a ruthless dictator. This country needs a savior, but it is not Guervno. I live alone. I have a portable satellite telephone. And I sometimes meet my CIA contacts near the border. I know this country, speak the language, and move freely."

The team quietly listened as Henry spoke. Through all of their life experiences none of them had met a CIA agent, but now here they were in the jungles of Cortiza, rescued by a guerilla guard and a freelance operative.

Garrett couldn't help but ask why.

Henry responded, "A year ago, my wife was killed in an accident. I was devastated. I was a professor of psychology at a Midwestern university. I quit to take some time to deal with the loss of my wife. The chairman was kind enough to promise that I could return anytime I wanted. I heard from him last week. The offer is still open. I guess I'm about ready to go home. But as to why I am here, I wanted to make a difference. Maybe I've helped a little to keep Guervno from taking over the country. In the meantime, the CIA is supporting another man who is gaining in popularity."

"What will happen to the people here if Guervno wins?" Michelle interjected as she remembered the fate of the Canadians.

"We must not allow that to happen." Henry's voice was stern. Michelle knew she had hit a deeply responsive chord.

Henry returned to his story. "I've had plenty of time to meditate and to grieve the loss of my wife. At the same time, the people here have taught me much. Do you know how the jungle people stop a bad wound from bleeding? They use ants! — huge black ants, about an inch long with fierce, nasty jaws. They hold the ant next to the wound and the ant sinks his jaws into the skin. The bite stings terribly for a moment, but the acid seems to disinfect the wound. Then they snap off the ant's head and the jaws stay imbedded. Then another ant and another and soon, the wound is stitched together with a line of ant heads! Look at your wound, Kevin. That's a common tropical fungus that I put on your wound. It must contain a powerful antibiotic because it has wonderful healing properties. This jungle is a living pharmacy. I've got several boxes of herbs and potions to take back with me. In the States, they'll think I'm a quack or witch doctor. But I've seen these remedies work."

Soon the group warmed up to Henry, a strange combination of professor, CIA operative and medicine man. They told him of their recent ordeals, beginning with the plane trip. They also talked about themselves and found Henry to be an avid, intelligent listener. Henry asked few questions, but encouraged each to probe their lives in depth. He never offered advice, but made each person feel the importance of their experiences and feelings.

"Can we call home?" Gary asked Henry. "I know my family is worried, if I could just call to let them know I'm O.K."

"It is not safe Gary. But I assure you that both your family and your company know of your rescue."

Everyone looked at Henry with faces filled with confusion, fascination, and relief. What a burden Henry had just lifted. Someone, somehow had gotten word to their families!

"You will have all the answers you need in due time," Henry offered, "but for now we have more important things to cover. I have listened to each of your stories about your past and what you have learned during your last few days in the jungle. There will be a helicopter arriving in about 24 hours to take you home. You only have a few hours before you return to your previous lives. It is imperative that you evaluate this emotional experience."

They were eager to hear what this enigmatic and fascinating man had to say.

"First," he stated, "if you want to find true meaning in your life, you have to do several things. You must understand yourself. Why do you have the deep feelings that you have? Why is it that you know how you should act, but for some reason seem to do the opposite?"

"It's funny," said Gary, "but ever since we met at that lodge in the Sierra Nevadas, we have all been talking about ourselves. In those long days and nights at Guervno's camp, I probably shared more about myself than I had in my entire life. And now we're all talking to you, as if you were the Dali Lama. It's as if we have been deprived of personal communication and insight our entire lives, and now we feel a need to fill that void."

"It is not personal communication you have been missing, Gary, it is insight. I would ask that you return to your quarters. I have placed a journal there for each of you. I spent several years developing the worksheets and activities. Even in this primitive place, I have given several copies to visitors. I would be honored if you would give it a try. It is divided into five sections, one section for each priority of your life. I would like for you to . . ."

"What five priorities of life?" Sharon interrupted, growing impatient. "And why is it so important that we do this for you?"

"It is not for me Sharon," Henry said in a calming voice. "It is for the five of you." As he looked around the group, he continued. "Each of you has been through a very significant emotional experience, which is one of the key factors in allowing you to undergo a permanent change. During the last few hours, you have all expressed to me a desire to change. You all have an incredible opportunity to turn your experience into a lifetime transformation. This process is the first step. If any of you feel you are doing this for me, don't participate in this exercise. It is only for those who are truly ready."

"Significant Emotional Experience, is that what you said Henry?" Gary asked, intrigued by Henry's words. Maybe this was his chance to change.

"Yes," Henry replied, "it is one of the few things that can impact an adult's character or personality after the age of eight."

"I know!" Gary responded enthusiastically. "My psychology professor, Dr. Gates, used to talk about SEEs in class!"

"I would like to hear about the five priorities Henry," Kevin said.

Chapter

31

The Five Life Priorities

Spiritual
Physical
Relationships
Mental
Financial

The team, including Sharon, listened intently as Henry continued. "Spiritual first," answered Henry. "Then physical, relationships, mental and finally financial. I have goals in each of these areas. Whenever I'm faced with a conflict among any of these priorities, I choose the higher one.

That is why it is important for you to go through this journaling process. You must evaluate each area before you begin change. Once you have done that, it won't take long for me to teach you these categories and show you how to construct your own priorities. It's only when you can start living according to your true priorities that the 'void' Gary spoke about filling will disappear."

"How do you know where to start?" Michelle asked. "I'm not sure I have something to write in all of those areas."

"The key is to just begin with the principles." Henry answered in a reassuring voice.

"What do you mean by 'principle?'" Gary asked.

Chapter 32

Henry on "Principles"

Henry began, "We are all very complex, but I will do my best to make it simple. A principle is a universal truth that always works when applied. It is like a principle of physics. Once we know the principles involved, we can calculate the next lunar eclipse or how long it will take a beam of light to reach Jupiter. There are principles, or laws, of nature too. There are causes and effects in chemistry. There are principles in mathematics that we apply all the time like the relationship of the radius of a circle to its circumference. Well, there are constants — principles — in human behavior as well. And if there are truly key principles of life, principles we can learn and then apply, just imagine what people could do."

Gary, sitting back and listening intently, was fascinated that he had retained so much of his psychology class.

"Henry's about to tell us the missing keys!" Gary exclaimed. "My weight, you know, what we talked about in the jungle, patterns, history repeating itself, *the keys!*"

Everyone, including Henry, laughed at Gary's enthusiasm.

"Let me give you an example. I have found this principle to be valid. R squared plus A squared equals success. That is Clement Stone's formula that simply means, if you can recognize, relate, assimilate and apply principles, you will find success," Henry smiled. Kevin looked a bit skeptical. Henry was not discouraged.

"Let me put this another way," Henry said, trying to respark Kevin's interest. "First, you have to know yourself; that is why journaling is so important. Through that process you will begin to identify your strengths and weaknesses. You must try as honestly as possible to describe the full range of your abilities and shortcomings. It has been said by many that 'faint ink is better than a strong memory.' Writing down your thoughts, fears, and dreams clarifies them. Clarity is the first key.

"Second, you must understand how those thoughts, fears and dreams affect your life and how you relate to others. Third, you must learn to recognize the principles that have been proven, relate them to your circumstance, internalize them, and apply them to achieve success. We're getting a little ahead of ourselves here, so let's go back to your journals. Several hours remain before dinner. I would like for each of you to begin capturing your thoughts in your journal. You have been given an opportunity to begin again, a second chance at life. To help you with this process I would like to offer one closing thought: if you had a magic wand, what would your life look like within each priority?"

With that, Henry stood and walked away. The team sat silently pondering the insights Henry had laid before them. When they returned to their beds, their new journals were waiting, just as Henry had promised. Distracted by thoughts of home, it was difficult to complete the exercises Henry had outlined in the journals, but all five wrote until dinner.

The Inward Search

Henry prepared the evening meal, just as he had every other. He stood by the woodburning stove, listening to music through his headphones. Garrett walked over to him and gently tapped him on his shoulder. Henry removed his headphones.

"What are you listening to?" Garrett asked curiously.

"Baroque music," Henry replied.

"Baroque?" Garrett responded.

"Yes, largo tempo."

"I'm almost afraid to ask, but why?"

"At dinner tonight the group will have many questions about what they have learned today. The baroque music will help me in relating with Gary and perhaps, even you."

"What about Kevin and Michelle and Sharon?" Garrett asked, now even more puzzled.

Henry smiled at Garrett's confusion, "I'll explain after dinner."

The group ate dinner quietly, content to rest tired, bruised bodies and enjoying a respite from the stress of their ordeals. Afterwards, they vaguely remembered enjoying the indiscriminate meal. Henry finished eating first, Gary always noticed, and began the evening conversation.

"It is not necessary for you to share with me what you have learned today through your writings. I would simply like to offer the next step in the process. I encourage each one of you to take what you have written and establish your priorities. Rate yourself on a scale of 1 to 10 as to how well you are achieving your ideals, and then set goals that articulate where you want to be. All I'm suggesting is that each one of us can achieve our goals through a systematic application of universal principles. You have just begun the process of barrier-free thinking, so all of this I am sure still seems a little foreign. Just give it time. Remember, R squared plus A squared equals success."

"Do you have any other overriding principles that you believe in and use?" Michelle asked, warming to the stimulation of new thoughts.

"Ever since Socrates, philosophers have been saying, 'know thyself.' But the difficulty people seem to have is figuring out how to know ourselves. Modern science has helped. This is another key that Gary was excited about. We have learned a lot about how the brain works. Some of us are right-brain dominant. Others are left-brain learners. Our 'wiring' makes a huge difference."

"How do they know that?" Michelle asked.

"Stanford conducted a study several years ago where they used infrared photography of the heads of students doing different tasks. During simple math problems, the left sides of all the students' brains went into action. The infrared photos clearly showed higher temperatures on the left side of their heads. They were literally radiating measurable heat from the left side of their brains, through their mathematical problem-solving.

"For other kinds of problem-solving, however, an interesting thing happened. While all worked on the same activity, some showed strong left-brain dominance, others showed high right-brain activity, and others, mostly women, interestingly, showed a fairly equal balance between both sides or hemispheres. Yet most people don't have any idea how they process information. The question I would pose to you is, how can we plan our lives if we don't even know how we think?

"The other thing we need to know is how much we value ourselves. No one with a low self-worth is likely to achieve significant personal goals. But with self-knowledge and a high regard of self-worth, people can do amazing things. In fact, I believe that if we know enough about people, we can predict, with a high percentage of accuracy, how they will act in a given situation. This is powerful stuff."

Gary was sitting to the side intently focused on Henry's words. Kevin, who was sitting right next to him, was engrossed in the notes he was writing in his journal.

"Excuse me, was the last key you said 'knowing your self-worth?'" Kevin asked, anxiously awaiting Henry's response.

"Yes," Henry replied, smiling.

"Anything else?" Kevin wanted to know. He pondered the possibility that human behavior might actually operate on basic principles that could be understood, perhaps even quantified.

113

"I don't want to draw any sweeping conclusions, but if you don't mind, I would like to use several of you to make this point."

Everyone on the team nodded in agreement, fascinated to see how Henry would use them to represent the characteristics of the right and left brain.

"You have all been sitting and listening to the conversation. Garrett has written a few notes, but not many. Kevin has a list A, B, C, D, highlighting each major point that we have covered. Gary has been sitting, listening intently, with no written record or possibly even already dreaming of how he can use this information. In their simplest forms, these are all signs of right and left brain dominance. Gary is more right-brained, interested in the big picture and how it relates to everything else. Kevin wants specifics, no frills, step by step. Garrett is fairly balanced, writing down some of the specifics, while still focused on the larger concept.

"What does baroque music have to do with this?" Garrett asked.

"Well, for the rest of you who do not understand what Garrett is speaking about, let me fill you in.

"Before dinner I was listening to baroque music in largo tempo through my headphones. Garrett had asked what I was listening to and I told him I would explain after dinner. Baroque music, specifically largo tempo, is used to enhance the right brain, the creative side. I am left-brain dominant and therefore use baroque music to stimulate the right side of my brain. The reason I was listening before dinner was that several of you are right-brained and by stimulating my right side it would make it easier for me to communicate with you."

"Wow, this is exciting. What's next Henry?" Gary asked, consistent with his "big picture" realm of thinking.

Chapter 34

Passion, Discipline and Persistence

Henry continued, "To achieve extraordinary success in any of the five areas of your life, you must have three well-developed characteristics: passion, discipline and persistence. Passion is more than desire; it is a deep, persistent love for the thing you are passionate about. Sometimes I use the word 'compulsion' when I talk about passion, because the feelings are so strong. But compulsion is too negative a word. So now I use the concept of deep love. I'm not talking at all about sexual passion. I mean a deep love of science or literature, of a period of history or of quilts, of chemistry or golf, of classic cars or gardening."

"Or helping others, through my work," Garrett said enthusiastically.

"Yes, exactly," said Henry smiling, acknowledging that Garrett had found his passion.

"Of course, some passions can be negative and destructive. Just look at Hitler. But passion also drove a prodigy like Mozart to write music and Galileo to risk his life for science.

"The second characteristic, discipline, is lacking in most people. How many people do you know who have a genuine passion for golf, but don't have the discipline to practice every day? Finally, there is good old-fashioned persistence. Not genius or education or wealth — just plain old stubborn persistence. I like to refer to the simple, powerful words in Churchill's speech: 'never, never, never give up!' Again, most people lack persistence; in fact, they lack all three. It's sad but true."

As the evening conversation continued, Michelle began to get weary and pale. Henry examined her, determining she had a mild infection. He gathered several of his herbs together and made her a warm drink. Everyone retired to bed.

Another Rap at the Door

At dawn the next morning, Michelle awoke to the familiar rap at the door. She quickly got up and looked out the small window in the cabin door. As expected, it was Ytefas who quickly gave Michelle instructions. "I'll find Henry; you gather the others. I've got bad news."

Ytefas turned and left to find Henry. He knew it was common for Henry to be gone at dawn. Henry could usually be found behind the cabin, by a small stream which meandered through the jungle. He went there each morning for meditation and prayer. When Ytefas and Henry returned to the cabin, the team had gathered at the table.

"What has happened?" Garrett asked, trying to keep the group calm.

"The rescue helicopter has crashed," Ytefas began, "about 45 minutes from here."

Sharon began to cry. Garrett put his arm around her to comfort her as she buried her head into his chest.

Ytefas continued, "I have just come from the scene. Nobody survived the crash. I was able to retrieve some of the things on board." Then Ytefas explained he had rescued two large boxes. All of the electronics had been destroyed in the crash.

"Was it sabotage? Did Guervno see the crash? Did he see Ytefas? How are we going to get out of here?" The questions were swirling.

Henry began damage control. "Everything is going to be fine. I was contacted while I was with Ytefas at the stream. The crash was an accident. The CIA will delay sending another chopper. They want to be sure that Guervno doesn't locate us. We will have a few more days together, but I believe we will be safe."

Ytefas explained to the group that there were boxes of fruit and clothing outside that he had carried from the crash scene.

Everyone was delighted to see the containers of fresh fruit. They sat down to papaya, mangoes and small, sweet red bananas while Ytefas reassured everyone that he had not been followed.

"You will get home," Henry stated, "just a little later than any of us had hoped."

"Speaking of going home, Ytefas and Henry, how safe are we here?" Sharon asked. "I keep worrying about that."

"Guervno might be able to locate us, eventually," Ytefas replied honestly. "But it will not be easy and it will take time. Our rescue should be arriving in just a few days."

118

The Spiral Staircase

T he team washed and dressed for the day. Although there were no new pants, everyone was delighted to have a fresh clean shirt. After two weeks, it was time for new clothes. After dressing, everyone gathered. Ytefas asked the team what they had learned from Henry.

"We've learned about brains and priorities, principles and journals, jungle medicine and baroque music," various members of the group chimed in together.

"Being from the jungle," Ytefas laughed, "the spiral staircase concept was difficult for me to grasp, but Henry was patient."

Kevin added, "I know what a spiral staircase is, but I'm not sure how it relates to what we have learned. Henry, can you explain?"

119

"Yes, it is difficult to understand, if you are from the jungle, but Ytefas has been a model student. The concept will be much easier for those of you who have already seen a 'real' spiral staircase. Life is like a spiral staircase. We start at the bottom. Then as we grow, go to school, have new and different experiences, we climb step after step up the spiral. Very few people continue growing and climbing for a lifetime. Most people stop climbing, stop expanding their horizons. They don't have the passion, the discipline or the persistence to keep growing. They form opinions and stop listening. They give up on personal goals because they seem difficult to achieve. Some people are just afraid to explore realities beyond the comfort of what they know."

"Henry," Sharon asked, "is it fear that keeps most people from growing?"

"Yes, Sharon, fear is one of the factors. Think of a toddler trying to walk. He stands and falls over and over again without even understanding what drives him to keep trying. Sometimes he gets a bruise, but he keeps getting up, over and over. Most adults don't have that kind of determination. They remember the times they were hurt and stop taking risks. Henry Miller had a point when he said: 'All growth is a leap in the dark.' It takes courage to enter the darkness. People tend to get complacent or tired and pause to rest, and then they may never get up again. Sometimes, even one simple defeat can stop someone dead in their tracks and instead of trying a different approach, they simply give up. Gradually, they begin to lose what they have achieved. They actually descend the staircase.

"The more conspicuous ones become alcoholics or compulsive gamblers, drug addicts or worse. But millions of others just settle into a routine and accept their niche in life. Then, at some point, they begin to reflect on their accomplishments with regret. 'I wish I had gone to graduate school. If only I had taken that job offer.' There are a lot of resigned and bitter people who spend many unproductive hours wishing they had climbed a little higher. One of my favorite phrases is from Robert Browning: 'Thy reach should exceed thy grasp, else what's Heaven for?' Too many people stop reaching.

"But there are a few who never stop their quest to learn and achieve. They continue climbing. With each new step they see farther and farther horizons. They discover new worlds and new joys. Their thirst for knowledge, their passion, grows. They seek a better, higher quality of life. And the most exciting part is that they truly begin to discover themselves, the depth and breadth of possibility. They become what they have the potential of becoming.

"Imagine if most moths just gave up as caterpillars. They were perfectly content in chewing leaves. Maybe a few would grow big enough and molt enough times to become a cocoon. Then safe and warm in comfortable isolation, these few would spend their lives sleeping. But one in a thousand decided to take a calculated risk and emerge from the cocoon. They would discover beautiful wings growing magically from their bodies. And they could fly! Fortunately, caterpillars follow the principles of nature that intend them to become moths or butterflies. It is people who have learned they have free will and choice. They have to work at becoming what nature intended them to be. But without passion, discipline and persistence, they fall short. At best they live in safe cocoons, never discovering that they could have wings and fly."

"Henry," Kevin began with uncharacteristic emotion, "when I was a small boy, I had a butterfly garden. It was made of plastic with small slits in the sides so the emerging butterflies could get out. Inside there was a branch with two small cocoons. My mother told me to wait and watch what would happen, but I was impatient. One day while my mother was cooking, I opened the top and took out one of the cocoons. I opened it. The butterfly looked fully formed but, it died. It was supposed to come out but, it died."

"Kevin, a butterfly must develop in its own time, much like a person. We can help create the right environment, but we can't force the process people go through. The butterfly died because it wasn't ready. People will stop ascending the staircase if we force them to grow before they are ready. A little while ago I heard you say that you didn't know what passion was. But of the five people on your team, Kevin, you are the one who truly has pursued a lifelong passion, your beloved bugs. You feel guilty, because you haven't developed relationships and friendships, but I think you are about to hatch from your cocoon, spread your wings."

Kevin, visibly moved by his mentor, sat silently, deep in thought.

"What does it mean to have wings?" Henry continued. "What are we intended to be? Most of us never discover the answer to those questions. But when people do reach the high steps on the spiral staircase, they discover a great capacity for love and a depth of deep emotion. They truly learn to empathize, to experience not only their own emotions, but the full range of the emotions of others. They become the complete persons they were meant to become. It is not the safest place to be. The moth is much safer in its cocoon. But what a tragedy to never fly. Again, I refer to my friend Browning who said, 'Tis better to have loved and lost than never to have loved at all.'"

Chapter 37

What is Success?

G arrett asked, "What about success? I think it can mean a lot of things. How would you define it Henry?"

"Brian Tracy is one of the leaders in human potential," Henry responded. "Actually, Tracy teaches that there are six components of success. The first is inner peace. That means that a person is spiritually fulfilled and free of guilt. The second component is excellent health with boundless energy. Most Americans do not realize that a large majority of depression could be corrected through exercise. Third, a person must be self-actualized. To Tracy, that simply means that a person's values are congruent with his actions. Fourth, a successful person has mutually supportive, loving relationships. Successful people cannot have a victim mentality, they must accept full responsibility for themselves and their place in life. Fifth, a successful person is goal-directed. He has clarity of purpose and provides a service to himself and others. And finally, successful people have a financial peace. This certainly does not necessarily mean wealth. Gandhi had freedom from financial stress and yet had almost no personal possessions.

"In addition to Tracy's six components, I would add that success is something each individual decides for himself. Success and happiness are in direct proportion to your personal and professional development. In other words, an adult cannot be truly successful and happy without continuing to develop, or to use a previous metaphor, without continuing to climb ever higher on that spiral staircase."

"I have to admit," said Garrett, "that everything you say makes sense. But at the same time, these ideas seem so foreign. How about if we take a break and try to digest some of this information and then start again. I really want to know more about the wiring of the brain. I want to know for sure if I am 'balanced' as you say. And I want to know more about self-concept. How can we measure something like that? But right now, my head is spinning."

The others agreed, thankful that Garrett had spoken for them. All five were fascinated by this man and his stimulating ideas. But they could only handle so many new ideas at one time. While they ate lunch, they talked among themselves and clarified some of the concepts. Suddenly it hit Garrett like a bright light. "What is wrong with us? It's like we've been in some time warp. We've spent all this time talking about ourselves and forgotten everyone back home."

"You have all been fighting for your lives. You haven't had time to worry about your families," assured Henry. "Besides, there is nothing you can do right now. We have no communications. Until the helicopter picks you up, it is not safe to use my satellite telephone. We certainly can't risk the chance of Guervno discovering that you are soon to be rescued. Your families all know that you are safe and that you will soon be on your way home. As soon as you are safely out of the country, you can talk to your families. Until then, try not to worry."

After lunch the group rested. Then Garrett, as was now customary, asked Henry to continue. Kevin suggested that they move outside to some fresh air and the group eagerly agreed. The cabin was growing claustrophobic. Henry agreed a bit reluctantly, cautioning his new friends to avoid the open areas.

Chapter

Quantum Leaps Up the Staircase

Knowledge
Significant Emotional Experience
Action

They found a shady spot under a huge tree and stretched out in the lush, damp grass. Everyone appreciated the welcome respite from the cabin while Henry continued. "The next concept I want to share is that to make quantum leaps up the staircase, three things need to be present: knowledge, a significant emotional experience and action. Let's talk about knowledge. It is everywhere and yet nowhere. Only 3 percent of Americans own library cards and 76 percent did not read a book last year. Less than 3 percent have written life goals. I could go on, but I'm sure you get my point."

"Henry, what does that say about people like me?" Michelle inquired. "I haven't read a book in probably five years."

"It means that at least in one area of your life you have stopped growing," Henry responded, in his usual direct way. There really is little difference between someone who is illiterate and someone who chooses not to read. I have a feeling that you are ready to emerge from your cocoon very soon and part of your upward journey will be spent in the library.

"The second way to make a great advance up the spiral staircase is through a significant emotional experience. Remember that 80 percent of most people's lives are determined by our attitudes and beliefs that were established when we were eight years old. We simply live out the script that was written when we were in second grade. It takes an emotional blast, a highly-charged emotional experience to shake someone out of this script. It isn't easy for someone to say, 'Hey, I don't want this to be my life.' A significant emotional experience, or SEE, can be a divorce, a near-death experience, the sudden death of a loved one, a financial disaster, or maybe an escape through the jungle," Henry grinned.

The group laughed, their outlook lightening in the fresh air and sunshine.

"But even with knowledge and a significant emotional experience, you are not going to make much progress up that spiral staircase unless you take action. The moth has no choice. It moves from caterpillar to cocoon to adult by the laws of genetics. But we have free will. We can decide to stay in the cocoon, some comfortable stage in our development. When you were all in danger, you let Ytefas lead you through the jungle to safety.

You reacted. That is good, but it is not good enough. When you go home and are out of harm's way, you have a choice: to continue in your current lives, or to become proactive and make changes, setting goals and then adopting a plan of action to achieve those goals. Your journaling will be key; you must continue the inward, and upward, search!"

Left-Brain; Right-Brain

The team was beginning to feel like school children, excited by the simple change in pace of learning. Gary remembered back to one day in junior high when on a beautiful spring day the class had convinced the teacher to have class outside. Learning was just more fun when the setting changed. The danger of Guervno was fading from their minds.

"Now let's get back to the topic I like to call 'brain wiring.' The function of the brain is still one of the great uncharted wildernesses. Just a few decades ago, scientists had identified a dozen or so chemicals secreted by the brain. That was exciting news. The brain was an organ and also a gland. As we have begun understanding some of the functions of chemicals like endorphin, we have discovered well over a thousand more chemical compounds! And we don't have a clue how most of these chemicals affect us. We do know that nicotine triggers the brain to release a substance called dopamine, essential to normal nerve activity. It seems that for cigarette smokers, heightened levels of dopamine give a feeling of well being. Still, brain chemistry is in its infancy."

"Whoa," Sharon interrupted, "I can feel your passion for this subject, but please give us novices a chance to breathe!"

"Please forgive me," Henry said, laughing that infectious laugh that never failed to brighten spirits. "I'm glad you can see my passion, but I didn't mean to overwhelm you! Just let me know when you are ready to continue."

"It's just all so new!" Sharon added, "It's like you are speaking a foreign language. My financial reports don't ever cover the wiring of the brain. Go ahead, I'll try to keep up."

"O.K, but only if you say so," Henry answered, with a smile on his face.

"A bit more advanced is our understanding of how different parts of the brain function. We know, of course, that the left lobe controls most of the right motor skills and vice versa. An interesting exception is eyesight. But we also know that certain types of thinking tend to occur in one or the other hemisphere. The left side of the brain is the computer, literal and logical. The right side is the feeling, emotional, intuitive, creative side. To function at your best, you need a combination of both sides. There is a bridge across the two lobes of the brain called the *corpus callosum* connecting the cerebral hemispheres and allowing the so-called 'two brains' to communicate with each other. Most people show some dominance, either left-brain or right-brain. Some people have very pronounced hemispheric dominance. An extremely right-brain dominant person might have pronounced artistic or musical ability, yet be unable to spell or do simple computations.

"A left-brain dominant person is usually a very punctual person and good with details, but may find small talk an effort and have to work at relaxing. I could talk all night about this fascinating subject; it is truly one of my passions because it gives clues to human behavior." Henry turned and again smiled at Sharon.

"I've read all the published articles I can find about people who have had their *corpus callosum* severed. It used to be a treatment for some epileptics. Others had it severed through wartime injuries. Without the *corpus callosum*, the two hemispheres operate independently. In one bizarre case, a man was fighting his wife with his left hand and trying to stop the fight with his right. When you get home, I recommend you read Ned Herrmann's book, *The Whole Brain Business Book*. It is the best I have read on the subject. It is comprehensive yet very readable. You can start applying the concepts with just a basic knowledge. I've given you an overview that will suffice until you have time to study in more depth."

"What are you Ytefas?" Garrett asked curiously. "Left or right-brained?"

"The same as you." Ytefas responded.

"What is that exactly?"

"Fairly balanced on both sides."

The group smiled. Gary interjected, "I don't think we understand all this stuff, but it sure is fun."

"On a scale of 1-10, Guervno is a nine left brain," Ytefas volunteered.

With the mention of Guervno, the group snapped back to reality. Until they were safely on that helicopter, no one could relax for long. Henry took over again. "Let's go back to the sides of the brain. As I said, most people show some dominance of one hemisphere over the other, but use both sides of the brain. Women tend to have a better balance between the two hemispheres. In fact, 80 percent of all the extreme dominant profiles are men. That may be why most of the children with perceptual handicaps and dyslexia are boys whose right brains dominate to the detriment of the left. The left brain, in general terms, is sequential, orderly. Left-brain dominant people see the world as it is. They pattern the world in formulas and grids and like to have everything in its place. These people like order, they like schedules and charts. They get things done in an orderly fashion. And they have a big advantage in school where there is a premium on left-brain education.

"Then there are those creative right-brain thinkers. They don't care much about time or neatness or organization. They like to visualize in concepts and leave the details to others. They are artistic, creative and musically-inclined. The phrase 'thinking out of the box' was coined for them. They love to dream and imagine, always striving to find new solutions. Where the left-brain person uses logic and reason, the right-brain counterpart uses emotion, feeling and intuition. If you are lost and want directions, the left-brain person will draw a map to scale. The right-brain person will remember landmarks, shapes and colors and sounds. If you want to know the emotional impact of a movie, a right-brain person will tell you about the music and the landscapes, the colors and the sounds and the places that evoked tears.

"We all know the maxim that birds of a feather flock together. Well, it seems that right brains tend to flock together in churches, vocations, clubs and friendships. And the same is true, of course, of the left brains. And there is a third group, those with a nice balance of both sides who tend to form relationships with each other. For some reason, there are many more men in the left-brain category than women. Perhaps that is why we see male dominance in math and engineering and applied sciences. And there are more women in the right-brain category, which may explain why so many women excel in arts and crafts and music and even the nurturing of children."

"How does the brain get wired one way or the other?" Garrett asked.

"That remains the $64,000 question. Where people are fairly balanced, nurture plays a part. But strong dominance is almost always demonstrated at a very early age, just as right or left-handedness, and appears to be irreversible without a traumatic illness or injury. The point is that balance, or hemispheric dominance, is neither good nor bad. Right-brained children, however, often struggle in traditional schools, because education stresses left-brain skills so heavily. Basic reading and phonics, math, memorizing dates and names and places and things — these are all left-brain skills. Kids who do poorly in music and art can usually get through school just fine. But kids who struggle with the three Rs, the so-called 'basics' have a miserable time in school. Schools nurture and reward left-brain learners, even if they are deficient in right-brain skills. But the penalty is harsh for kids who are deficient on the left side."

"Don't teachers study this information?" Kevin asked. "I know my middle son really struggled in school and I thought it was just because he was lazy! Are you saying it could have been that he is just 'wired' in a different way than the school teaches?"

"Yes, he could simply be 'wired' differently, and no, most traditional schools and teachers don't study right and left brain. Most of the information is so new, it just hasn't made it to the educational field. One influential book that actually made the best-seller list is *Drawing on the Right Side of the Brain*. And a woman named Barbara Vitale has written several books about teaching right-brain dominant children. But there is such a strong movement toward academic competencies, that in many school districts, the arts are being displaced with an even greater emphasis on the 'three Rs.' I've got nothing against accountability and academic goals, but these need to include music, art and drama, or our right-brain dominant children face a losing battle.

"Most of you are fortunate. You may have a strongly dominant hemisphere, but you still have effective resources in both lobes. Still, it could be a great benefit to you if you understood how your brain is wired, as well as knowing the strengths and weaknesses of others. Let me give you an example. Say you have a strong left-brain dominance. You tend to see the world in terms of black and white, right and wrong. You may be decisive and opinionated, intolerant of others who disagree with your obviously logical and correct point of view. You tend to be judgmental.

"Now let's say you are married to a predominately right-brain thinker. Your spouse may see the world in infinite gradations of gray tones and multiple valid points of view. The world is not logical at all, but subject to feelings, and those feelings are always shifting with circumstances. These two people may be deeply in love, but imagine how difficult it is for them to communicate or to sustain a long-term relationship unless they both understand their differences and learn to use this information to their advantage.

"The good news is that right-brain and left-brain thinkers need each other, in the workplace, in marriages, in society. Both sides bring powerful strengths. But too often they come into conflict. They become adversaries. They threaten each other's sense of values. They just don't understand each other. We don't blame a cardinal for being red or a jay for being blue, but many of us blame others who don't think the way we do.

"Even worse, in my opinion, are those people who are at war with themselves. A right-brain father may have been a great musician and started pushing his young left-brain daughter to follow in his footsteps. The daughter adores her father, but on a scale of 1-10, has 1 point on the right side and 10 on the left. She is a prodigy in math and science, logic and languages, but hopeless in the arts and music. She grows up miserable, disappointing her doting father who can't understand how he could raise a daughter without musical talent. Still, the daughter struggles and struggles, practicing the piano mechanically and learning hundreds of compositions by heart. She even learns to play competently, but never with expression or passion. Worse yet, she hates every minute at the keyboard and may feel she has failed to meet her father's expectations.

"I really encourage you to understand yourselves better. Find out where your strengths lie and use them for your own personal development. Find out your weaknesses as well and learn to minimize their impact on you. Learn to appreciate who you are as well as who you are not. Too many of us are mortified by our weaknesses. At the highest levels of the spiral staircase, we learn to celebrate the fullest development of our gifts, and then to be content with the result. I like to think that a moth rejoices when it emerges from a cocoon, and doesn't look around thinking, 'I sure wish I looked like that butterfly.'"

40

Chapter

Where is Guervno?

enry decided he had talked long enough, but his new friends were fascinated. They wanted to find out more about their own strengths and weaknesses. They all wanted to know about their hemispheric dominance and exactly how they were "wired" as Henry called it. They could hardly wait to read more and to take some of the tests that identified and measured hemispheric dominance. In the meantime, they urged Henry to continue.

Henry was excited by the interest of the group, but thought it was necessary to open a new topic. "There is an abundance of knowledge available for each of you to learn, but the process of understanding yourself is just as important as the information. If you do not know yourself, the information will be useless. I want each of you to achieve your life goals. For that to happen, you must continue your inward search. Please return to your journals. Begin trying to understand how you think and why. Explore your childhood — the kinds of friends you chose. I have many evaluation exercises for you to complete that will help you to understand yourself and your priorities. As you begin to formulate a clear picture of yourself, you will have a baseline from which to begin setting goals.

"Tomorrow, we will come back together to discuss the subconscious picture we hold of ourselves; but for now, use this solitude to learn and grow."

As the five stood, Henry warned them to remain close to the cabin until they retired for the evening.

"Any word from the States?" Ytefas asked Henry.

"None," Henry replied. "I'm sure we will hear from them soon. How much time do we have?"

Ytefas looked at Henry, "Maybe 24 hours, but I can't be sure. My sources are reliable, but Guervno is ruthless, determined and resourceful. The sooner you depart, the better!"

"We must stay here," said Henry, "There is no other place for the helicopter to land. Is there anything to be gained by alarming the others?"

"No. Keep them focused and close to the cabin. Pray for the 'copter's quick arrival. I must return to the jungle. I know that Guervno is searching for us, but I hope to return with good news."

With that, Ytefas was off.

Henry sought out each of the five team members to insure they were all accounted for.

Michelle was lying on her bed, unfocused and despondent. She was not even aware of Henry's arrival.

"What's wrong?" Henry asked.

"I'm scared Henry. I don't know why, but I have a growing sense of anxiety. I have often had premonitions of danger, and very often they proved to be justified. Sometimes I have dreams. I dreamt of danger on the plane to Cortiza. Sometimes I just have a strong feeling that something is about to happen. I can *feel* it, Henry. Something bad is getting closer to us. I don't know if it's Guervno or just me. I can't really describe it, but I have learned to pay attention to my premonitions. And I dearly miss my husband and my girls. Henry, will I ever get home?"

"Michelle, there are some questions only God can answer. Your fear of Guervno is certainly justified. You know from experience he is an evil man. Ytefas has gone back into the jungle to locate him. Guervno has never been able to locate my cabin, but we must continue to be extremely careful. The CIA is sending another helicopter to rescue us. Right now we need to focus on what we can control. It is not productive to simply sit and worry. Prayer may comfort you. You are a strong person; look at what you have survived thus far. Remember, the last 5 percent of this experience and of our own growth will be the most difficult. Try to look within, stay positive. Ytefas will do everything he can to insure our safety."

Chapter 41

Self-Esteem

T he next morning, Henry gathered the team back together after breakfast to continue talking. He and Michelle
had agreed that they would not share her concerns with
the other team members. After having an evening of solitude,
everyone, including Michelle, had a glow of refreshing new
insight about themselves. Gary and Sharon had found the
reflection difficult, but felt a great sense of gratification for
having completed the process.

"Let's talk about self-esteem," Henry said. "I've already mentioned the importance of self-esteem in achieving goals and what
some people call self-actualization. When you return home, I recommend you study Maxwell Maltz's classic *Psycho-Cybernetics*
and Jack Canfield's tape series *How to Build High Self-Esteem.*

Here's an overview. I think we are born with an innate need to feel good about ourselves. At the same time, we come into the world with what Locke called a *tabula rasa*, a blank slate. We are empty vessels, ready to be filled with knowledge and experience. Given a safe and loving home, most young children feel that the whole world loves them. I still remember when my five-year-old announced, 'I think the whole world loves me!' That is the epitome of healthy self-esteem.

"But something happens to most of us as we begin experiencing our lives. Despite our innate need to feel positive self-esteem, or perhaps because of that need, most of us grow up feeling inadequate. We begin suffering the slings and arrows of outrageous fortune. We experience hurt and betrayal. We become disillusioned by the reality that no one is perfect. We discover that the whole world does not love us. Some psychologists estimate that an alarming 90 percent of the population has deficient self-esteem.

"Yesterday, I asked each of you to begin the process of evaluating your own view of yourself. Self-esteem is simply our own valuation of worth or self-concept. We think we are clumsy, fat, unattractive, bossy, crabby, ignoble. We do 10 good things a day and remember the one instance where we lost our temper or said something stupid. We play a hundred notes correctly on a musical instrument and remember the one we missed. We forget the compliments we received all day at work and remember that one unkind or thoughtless criticism. We focus on that one rude driver who cuts us off on the freeway. All these negatives accumulated day by day make us think less of ourselves and of others. The poet e.e. cummings has a beautiful line I often used in my classes: 'Nothing which we are to perceive in this world equals the power of your intense fragility.' I think he was writing about a newborn, but it isn't a bad description of adults either. Our self-concepts are intensely fragile.

"In fact, our self-worth, generally speaking, is so fragile and vulnerable, that it takes 50 examples of praise and encouragement to offset a single criticism. What chance do we have in a marriage, for example, or in the workplace, when it takes 50 encouragements to offset one negative, or perceived negative? And that unfair 50 to 1 ratio is even more perverse than it sounds, because studies show if the same praise comes from the same person, the value of that praise tends to diminish over time. That means if a husband constantly tells his wife that she looks beautiful, or even that he loves her, the impact of his statements gradually diminishes over time. So the people closest to us have to work harder and more creatively all the time to build and maintain our self-esteem.

"Even with nurturing parents and teachers who spend so much time with us shaping our sense of self-worth, most of us grow up with very little self-confidence. We do not think of ourselves as lovable, attractive, or even basically good. And we started getting into this negative rut as very young children. By the time we are eight years old, 80 percent of our self-worth has been determined. Now think how many times you spilled your milk, wet your bed, broke something, forgot to bring home something from school, lost something and were told 'no' in even the most loving of homes.

"How can a parent hope to keep up that impossible 50-1 ratio of praise to criticism? And even if we do all the right things, how can we be sure that our children perceive their lives to be positive? It is very difficult to evaluate or measure a person's self-worth. Even as children, we tend to bury our concept of ourselves deep within us in our most private and personal thoughts. Since we cannot see self-concept in others, we look for external clues. We look at behavior and try to interpret it. The best test I know of is called the Tennessee Self-Concept Scale, and it requires a trained professional to do the interpretation.

"Let me give you just one example of why it is so difficult to evaluate another person's self-worth. Take the hypothetical Ms. Smith. She dresses beautifully and drives a new Mercedes. She sells 100 homes a year: the perennial top real estate agent in the city. She is attractive, articulate and competent. Her picture is often in the paper receiving an award for her accomplishments. You get the idea. You'd think her picture would be in the dictionary next to the entry 'self-worth.' But it is entirely possible that Ms. Smith is driven to success by her low self-esteem. And even though she is successful in conspicuous and tangible ways, it may also be true that all these rewards still fail to fill some internal void. The fact is, external indications of self-esteem are often erroneous. Many conspicuously successful people like actors, politicians and entrepreneurs fall into this category. High achievement is sometimes a symptom of deficient self-worth, especially if these achievers are constantly attempting to prove themselves.

"We certainly know of people who turn to drugs and alcohol searching for that elusive sense of self-worth. Others join clubs and societies and gangs to find self-worth, seeking the company and approval of others. The need for approval is one of our most powerful motivators. I have found the simplest test of a person's self-worth to be whether a person is basically positive or negative. Want to find a person with a solid foundation of self-worth? Look for someone who laughs when someone else relates a humorous story. Look for someone who loves the spring sunshine and the new flowers. Someone who encourages others and thanks them. Someone who apologizes for an offense, even if fault was mostly on the other side. Someone who volunteers without expecting public recognition. Someone who delights in seeing others succeed. Someone who can be content alone reading a book or working on a hobby.

"The good news is that adults can make progress in building their sense of self-worth. We can discover our fascination with a topic like renaissance music or early American crafts, and study it because it simply gives us pleasure. We can learn the joys of celebrating our own imaginations. We can learn to be increasingly responsible for our own happiness, instead of relying on the approval of others. We can discover that self-worth is never served when we try to bring others down, but only when we climb up our own spiral staircase. We can discover the things that bring us joy and set goals to achieve them. It begins with a deep understanding of ourselves and our needs. Then we need to learn to accept ourselves and to celebrate our abilities. One of my favorite quotations is by Scriabin: 'The universe resounds with the joyful I Am!'. When you go home, you have a lot of studying to do! I hope I will be able to keep track of your progress."

With these words, Henry seemed to be ending the day's session. They were expecting another journal session and really didn't feel like writing on such a glorious day. Besides, Henry was not only an engaging speaker, he also kept their minds distracted from the dangers they still faced from Guervno. Sharon surprised herself by taking the initiative to ask Henry if he would be willing to move the group outside and talk a bit about spirituality. The team sat down under their "teaching tree," as Michelle had named it and Henry continued.

Chapter 42

Spirituality

Henry began, "I believe that we are all spiritual beings having a physical experience." Since I have been recommending books for you to read, I'd add to your list Gary Zukav's *Dancing Wu Li Masters* and Richard Foster's *Celebration of Discipline* for starters. If I'm right about our spiritual nature, then we must find our spiritual base. We must get in touch with our spiritual side. Although I invdividually believe in God, I'm not talking religion, certainly not any traditional organized denomination. But a religious community may be the easiest way for most of us to begin accessing our spirituality."

Kevin said, "I know this may be changing the subject a bit, but why do you think I'm unable to handle an intimate relationship?

Is it because I have always denied my spiritual side? I know from your discussions of the brain that I must be pretty far on the left side. I've always been analytical and I hate small talk. Now I realize that small talk is the way many people build relationships. To me, it always seemed such a stupid waste of time. I never had time for anyone who wasn't logical or rational. My wife keeps saying that I need to understand the feelings of my boys. Just my luck, my wife and boys are probably all right-brain people! I don't think I'm ever going to get to the spiritual dimension if I can't even form relationships with people I see every day."

Henry turned on his warm, enigmatic smile that the group had learned to know and found so endearing. "Kevin, you have come so far, so quickly. You have a deep hunger to learn. And I know you love your wife and sons. But you are one of those people I was talking about who needs to start with building a self-concept. You're a brilliant engineer. But your intellect, by itself, cannot get you to the highest levels of that spiral staircase I keep talking about. I know you have a deep hunger to bond with people. I've seen you establish some pretty close friendships in the last few days. And you have become a trusted leader. Now it may be time to continue that progress, perhaps with some professional counseling and certainly by continuing to nurture these new friendships. Actually, I'd be pretty careful about my advice to get counseling. The majority of counselors probably need more help than you do," Henry laughed.

"It will be a long journey to understanding, but I promise you it will be worth every bit of the effort. There will be pain and frustration, but nothing like the ordeal you've been through in the past few days. If you will permit me a bit of advice," Henry continued hesitantly, "I'd recommend you begin with your wife. Sit down and talk. Tell her you love her. Explain about your left brain and how you're beginning to realize that she needs much more that you have been able to give her in the past. There was a reason you two were drawn together. Build on that strength. Go for it! One more thing, Kevin," Henry said thoughtfully. "You might think about this quote from William Blake, 'Everything that lives, lives not alone, nor for itself.'" The group sat silently for a moment, and then Henry continued.

"The five of you certainly have had a significant emotional experience. That's a great start. Your life is ahead of you. Get the information you need; it is readily available. Then put your knowledge into action. Remember, passion, discipline and persistence are the three keys. This is a special chance of a lifetime to change your life."

43

Chapter

Rescue!

They sat sprawled under the teaching tree, focused on Henry's words. But, as he began to speak, they heard it: the unmistakable, rhythmic "chop, chop, chop" of a helicopter. For a moment, the team was unsure of what was happening. Then the SH60 SeaHawk cleared the mountain directly in front of them. Every eye was fixed upon the helicopter, and just when they were ready to shout for joy, they realized a gunman was kneeling in the open door in the ready position. The aircraft was hanging directly over the cabin now, and the man in fatigues opened fire. It took a moment to realize that his gunfire was directed toward the nearby jungle, and that gunfire was being returned.

"Inside the cabin!" Henry shouted, trying to head everyone out of immediate gunfire.

As they entered the cabin, Ytefas ran in behind them. "Guervno is here!" he shouted. "The gunner is attempting to hold them off. When the helicopter lands, you've got to get on as fast as you can. It can't set down long; Guervno's men are too close! Be prepared to jump!"

"Aren't you coming with us?" Sharon asked, fearing the answer.

"No," Ytefas replied, "My work is here; you must go!"

The staccato of gunfire from Guervno's troops underscored his words.

"Run!" shouted Ytefas.

Gary surprised the team as he sprinted toward the descending helicopter faster than anyone would have believed. He shouted, "I hope I don't have to jump!" but his words were swallowed in the approaching whirlwind of noise and dust and leaves.

Gary's action galvanized the others who scrambled toward the landing area in disorganized panic. The men passed Gary whose breathing was suddenly labored. Gary stopped for a moment, bent over, his hands resting on his knees. Garrett looked back at the deserted cabin and saw Sharon. She was simply standing, frozen in terror.

"I'm scared!" she screamed, covering her ears from the blast of automatic weapons.

"We've got to go *now!*" Garrett shouted. "They're about to land!" He ran back to Sharon, who hugged him with the desperation of someone drowning. For a moment, Garrett thought she would collapse and he would have to carry her. He had to forcefully break her terrified embrace. Then, his arm around her waist, he yelled, "Come on! We're going home!" Then they began running.

The gunfire grew louder as the SeaHawk started to land. The team moved into its wind wash, which blew a fury of red dust, blasting their skin, lashing into their eyes and tugging at their clothing. Michelle screamed as she nearly lost her footing in the stinging whirlwind. Everyone ducked and closed their eyes against the onslaught of debris. For a moment the helicopter lifted and Gary panicked, screaming, "Noooo! Don't leave us!" his voice disappearing in the maelstrom. Then the chopper dropped into the clearing. Everyone knew this was the moment of truth. If they didn't make it, their death was certain.

It seemed miles across the small clearing, and they seemed to be running in the same slow motion of a nightmare. The forever of the moment lengthened as each member realized clearly the absolute finality of the stakes. They stumbled, struggling to keep their eyes open in the choking red dust. Suddenly Michelle realized that she had left her journal behind. Even as she struggled the last hundred feet to the helicopter, she found herself sobbing at the loss. What a thing to think about she mused as she reached the chopper just behind Kevin and Henry. Immediately she was snatched in by powerful arms. One by one the team members scrambled into the helicopter. As Garrett was pulled aboard, he heard shots whizzing by, striking the metalwork. It was an awful sound. The sound of death.

Gary was 20 feet away when he fell. For a moment Henry feared it was a heart attack and without thinking, he dropped from the open doorway and ran to his friend. But Gary was quickly on his feet again and moments later, Henry was back inside and hands were grabbing Gary's arms and shirt. He was hollering, but his voice was drowned by the gunfire and the revving of the engine. A bullet ricocheted off the door frame. As the helicopter began lifting, Gary hung helplessly at the door. Suddenly, uniformed troops appeared in the clearing. Sharon could see Guervno gesturing wildly to his troops as weapons concentrated their fire on the aircraft.

Desperate hands strained to pull Gary into the helicopter as it skimmed over the tops of trees. Kevin leaned farther out to grab Gary's belt and felt himself slipping head first from the doorway. For a moment, both teetered precariously in the open sky. Kevin now had a death grip with both hands on Gary's belt. He closed his eyes and prayed, determined to save Gary or die in the attempt. Then, inch by inch, he was pulled back to safety. He and Gary tumbled in just as the last of the earthbound gunmen fired off a last frustrated round of ineffective fire at the receeding SkyHawk.

"Thanks guys!" Gary managed to puff, realizing how inadequate those words sounded. They all rolled back, releasing him, breathing hard from their mad dash for life. Kevin was grimacing in pain. His shirt was ripped open revealing an angry scrape from his chin to his waist. No one mentioned his reckless heroics as Henry attended to the wound.

"Is anyone else hurt?" Henry asked, quickly surveying the cabin of the SkyHawk. He spotted three shell holes, but miraculously the helicopter and its crew were safe.

Almost in unison they looked at each other in disbelief, then out the doors into the jungle below, beautiful in its lush greenery. They absorbed the broad blue sky and the realization that they were truly safe. Faces broke into smiles and tears of relief and joy.

Then Michelle's brow furrowed, "Will Ytefas be alright?" she looked at Henry.

"I'm not sure, Michelle," Henry replied. "He is a dedicated man, but there is a price on his head. He has risked his life for what he believed was right. Still, he has proven to be very resourceful. I think the helicopter provided plenty of distraction for him to escape. We should all be very thankful."

A hush fell on the five Americans. They had come to love the courageous, simple man who had risked his life for them. They knew his life was in danger. They all remembered his parting words: "Do not worry about me, my friends."

"What will he do Henry?" Garrett asked.

"Ytefas knows Guervno. He knows his camps and where he has hidden his weapons. He knows his strategies and has even duplicated his communications code book. He is an excellent organizer and people seem to trust him. I think we will hear his name again if he can manage to elude Guervno. He said to tell you he would miss you, but he thinks he will meet all of you again. He hopes perhaps you will return to El Frando when the political climate is better. They need the El Frando plant to be successful. And one of his goals is to see the Golden Gate Bridge some day."

They lapsed into silence both from emotion and because of the noise of the chopper blades. Each of the five American corporate members entertained their own thoughts and concerns. Why can't life be simple? What will Guervno do next? Is my family O.K.? Does Ytefas really have a chance to help his country? Will the Americans help? When can I call home? Will Ytefas be safe?

Gary broke the silence. "Where are they taking us?"

"To the USS Sphinx stationed just off the coast," Henry answered. "The CIA wants to debrief all of you to find out all you know about Guervno."

"But we don't know anything," Sharon complained. "We only saw him twice . . .well, three times if you count the clearing. I just want to go home!"

Henry told the group how important it was to meet with the CIA. Guervno was planning a coup in the near future, and their information might help save the country from a devastating revolution. He reassured the group that he would be allowed to stay with them except when they were individually being questioned. To lessen their fear, he gave them an overview of what they would be asked. "The government knows what you have been through; they will make your debriefing as quick and painless as possible."

Growing weary from shouting over the noise and from their ordeals, they sat in silence as the helicopter sped them across Cortiza. Soon the coastline appeared and they began flying over the ocean. The suddenly expanded, uninterrupted horizon seemed to have symbolic significance to them. Each marveled at the beauty of the vista, and reflected that they had at moments despaired from seeing such a sight again. Then they spotted the sleek lines of the USS Sphinx. "Ohhh!" breathed Sharon, "do you think we could shower?" No one answered, but each of them visualized the raw luxury of a simple, hot shower in untainted water!

They hovered only briefly moving in to the landing, and the capable pilot kissed the deck with obvious skill. Everyone moved eagerly to disembark onto the reassuring safety of an American vessel, each acutely aware of the significance of that thought after their recent confinement. They stood somewhat shakily and breathed the crisp sea air with relish. Their faces beamed in the sunshine as they nodded and shook hands with the greeting party. While there was a polite reserve characteristic of those in the military, the officers and crew seemed genuinely proud to be part of a successful rescue. The team found an unexpected solace in the orderliness of the ship. It was a stark change from the dank and dangerous jungle! As Henry had promised, the debriefings were short. Soon the SeaHawk was refueling while the team enjoyed hot soup and yeasty biscuits and thought of their next stop: home!

44
Chapter

Home

"Home." Gary said. "Right now there is no sweeter word."

The group agreed. The last two weeks had been an incredible journey: the retreat house, the train, kidnapping and escape, Ytefas, Guervno and his gunmen, the CIA, Henry, the harrowing helicopter rescue. Through all their dreams of what "Team El Frando" would be, none of them could have imagined the reality they had experienced.

Now they were about to head home. Henry and the five members of "Team El Frando" reboarded the SeaHawk. They sat quietly and the blades began to spin.

Sharon reached out for Garrett's hand. "Thank you," she began, "for reaching out to me when we began this trip. You thought you needed my advice, but I think maybe God gave you to me to open my heart."

"I did need your advice Sharon," Garrett responded. "I have a great life, and now, thanks to you, and Henry and Ytefas, I have a second chance to get it all right, finances included."

Garrett reached out and held Sharon in a strong embrace. The once called "ruthless" Sharon had connected. This hug started a round of them among the team. It was only the beginning, but the journey had begun.

"We're going home," Michelle said in a quivering voice. "I can't wait to see my family, but I'm going to miss all of you. We're finally a team, just like Steve and Mary wanted!"

The team looked at each other, "Steve and Mary?" Gary said. "I almost forgot about them. It seems like years ago that we met them. I wonder if they know we're coming home?"

"Yes," stated Henry, smiling enigmatically, "they know."

"Are you sure?" Kevin asked.

"I'm sure," Henry responded, offering nothing more.

Before Kevin could pursue the subject, the pilot announced they were about to land at the San Jose Airport. The team looked out the windows. Their faces beamed at the sight of American soil.

"Look!" Gary shouted, "Our families are here!"

Sure enough, a few hundred feet from the helipad they could see their families standing in a large circle. Their hands were filled with balloons and banners. "Welcome Home" one banner proclaimed. "We love you" said the one from Gary's family.

Michelle spotted her girls waving a sign that read "To the world's greatest mom!" Garrett's wife was standing with a huge bundle of balloons of every color in the rainbow. She released them just as the helicopter landed. On the helicopter the men and women of Team El Frando burst into uncontrollable tears. Their joy and relief were too much to contain.

Garrett was the first off the SeaHawk. He ran to meet his wife who met him almost at the helicopter door. One by one the team climbed out, embraced by their families and ecstatic to be home. Even Kevin's wife had come to meet him. Sharon smiled when Kevin hugged her, lifting her off her feet. Two passengers remained on board for a moment. "Are you ready, Sharon?" Henry asked as they sat together, watching the blades wind to a stop.

"As I'll ever be," she replied. Then they got off together and walked across the tarmac into the terminal. Much to their surprise, Mary and Steve were there to meet them.

"Thank God you're home!" Mary said, choked with emotion.

"Thank God I went!" Sharon responded, surprising even herself as she smiled at Henry.

"I don't believe we have ever met, although you do look very familiar. My name is Steve." He reached out his hand to Henry.

"Henry James. I spent the last few days with your team."

Steve nodded distractedly in acknowledgment to Henry as he surveyed Sharon's appearance. She had had time to shower and eat a warm meal on the USS Sphinx. And her military-issue clothing was unexpectedly flattering. Still, she showed signs of her ordeal. She looked a little thinner, and had scratches on her forehead. The deep bruises on her shins were hidden by the fatigues, but a slight limp suggested her discomfort. Steve also detected something else, an air of confidence.

"Let this brave woman go home. She has been through a lot!" said Henry.

"Yes, yes, of course!" said Steve. "We will be in touch with you, Sharon, when you have had time to recuperate."

Mary murmured goodbyes, too, and Henry ushered Sharon out rather briskly.

Sharon turned away from their departure and to face Henry. "I want to take this moment to say how much you have helped me, and to thank you. You have changed my life, Henry!"

"Only you can change your life Sharon. I just offered some new insights," Henry replied.

"I hope our paths cross again," Sharon said.

"The choice is yours. Here is the number where I will be staying if you would ever like to call. I would be glad to work with you."

After the two embraced, Henry turned and left. In those few moments Team El Frando disbanded. The next day, with a little time to reflect on their ordeals, each member wondered when they might meet again.

45

Chapter

Sharon

Sharon was both too excited and too exhausted to relax when she arrived home. The experiences of the past few weeks were still overwhelming and had barely registered. What a whirlwind! she thought. She had been accepted as a consultant on Team El Frando, selected over the best candidates in the country. She couldn't help smiling at the thought. Then the unbelievable chain of events in Cortiza. And now, sipping a cup of tea from her favorite china cup, she wasn't altogether sure the ordeal had really happened. Then she fingered her TEF pin, a piece of jewelry she wore every day.

Her thoughts moved like swirling fog from one place to another. She remembered Henry's voice and how much those days of mentorship had meant to her. Then she thought of IMM and won-

163

dered what would happen to the El Frando plant. She felt a sudden stab of guilt about Duke Milligan, the man who had risked so much. I wonder what happened to him, she mused. Then she thought of Ytefas in the jungle with a band of guerrillas, trying to bring sanity to a country in ruins.

This had been a good experience, she thought. She had been terribly frightened, but she hadn't been harmed. And she had made some friendships that she was determined to nurture. She had certainly had her "Significant Emotional Experience!" Now what? Did all that talk about the spiral staircase really make sense? What about those promises she had made about changing her life when she got home? As she sipped the aromatic chamomile, her thoughts kept returning to Henry. She decided that she would try to look at her priorities.

Spirituality, she remembered, was the first priority for Henry. Spirituality, she thought wistfully. Every Sunday as a child she had sat in church with her parents. She had sung the hymns and recited the prayers. Sometimes she had even felt close to God. She remembered the winter when her little brother had been so sick with croup. She had feared for his life and had prayed fervently. She had even written a letter to God that appeared in the church bulletin.

She remembered kneeling on the cold wooden floor beside her bed and reciting, "Now I lay me down to sleep," her mother and father kneeling on either side of her. But gradually God had faded for her. By the time she was a teenager, she went to church just to please her parents, afraid to admit to them, or even to herself, that she was just reciting empty words. This was different, she thought, but where do I begin? She decided that she would do some research on spirituality. But one thing for sure, she thought, drinking another soothing sip of tea, she was not going back to Cortiza!

What was she going to do? After six weeks, she had to get back to work. At least IMM had been generous with the severance pay.

It wasn't a fortune to be sure. But it was a nice surprise, nevertheless. As she thought of returning to her work as a consultant, a wave of physical exhaustion swept over her again. Ever since her return, she had suffered these bouts of deep lethargy. Her doctor had told her to expect them for awhile. She had been through a trauma, and she needed some time to recover. As she slowly drifted into a deep sleep, Sharon felt two powerful thoughts. One was the disturbing feeling that her Cortiza experience was somehow not yet over. The other was the remembrance of Guervno's camp and Ytefas telling her that she was going to die, to be ambushed on the way back to the train. Ytefas had told all of them that they had only a few hours to live, so make their peace with God.

Then she heard the voice of Henry saying something about knowledge and action. She vaguely remembered the context as she drifted into a deeper, dreamless sleep. When she awoke, hours later, she didn't recognize her own bedroom at first. Then the fog slowly lifted and she realized she was safely home. As she sat up she came to a decision: she would find Henry and continue their discussions. After all, he had said, "Feel free to call if I can be of assistance." He had even given her his card. Imagine, having business cards after a year in the jungles of Cortiza! Henry had told her that he was going to retire from teaching and become a writer as well as spend some time with his younger brother.

Sharon picked up the phone. Moments later, she was talking to Henry as if they were lifetime companions. He would be delighted to meet with her and continue their discussions. He encouraged her to read two books before their meeting, books he had mentioned in the jungles of Cortiza: Foster's *Celebration of Discipline* and Zukav's *The Dancing Wu Li Masters*. Sharon said she wanted to explore her budding feelings of spirituality. They agreed on a time and place to meet in two weeks.

Sharon felt a surge of excitement as she hung up the phone. In some vague way, she felt she had begun to follow up on promises made in that faraway country. She found herself looking forward to meeting with Henry again. Maybe he would have some news from the others as well. She left the house feeling buoyant, and drove to her favorite bookstore. She realized as she entered that the only part of the bookstore she knew were the shelves on economics, financial planning and the stock market. "Time to expand my horizons," she muttered to herself and found an employee to help her. A short time later she was returning home with her two purchases and a deepfelt commitment to read both books carefully. Wouldn't Henry be pleased!

Two Weeks Later

Sharon arrived at the restaurant ahead of time, excited and looking forward to meeting with Henry. She was anxious to recount some of the experiences they had shared in Cortiza and to see what Henry would say about her awakening desire to become more spiritually grounded. Even though they had known each other for only a few days, Sharon ran to greet him as an old friend. She was completely comfortable in his presence and was anxious to ask him so many questions. Maybe, just maybe, he would consent to be her mentor and coach.

After they were seated and talked briefly about their escape, Sharon said, "Henry, I thoroughly enjoyed *Celebration of Discipline*. I found it to be enlightening and non-sectarian, and I look forward to putting into practice some of the things I learned, especially the discipline of solitude and prayer. But I don't understand how quantum physics relates to spirituality."

"I'm glad you enjoyed the book," Henry responded. "I have recommended it to hundreds of people and almost without fail I find that they thank me for putting them in touch with Richard. As far as *Dancing Wu Li Masters* and quantum physics, it is my belief, Sharon, that we are spiritual beings having a physical experience. Therefore, quantum physics tells us that at the subatomic level in all matter, there is nothing but energy and information. That's what *Dancing Wu Li Masters* is all about. Until we get in touch with that spiritual side of our humanness, we will always be feeling, to some degree, emptiness, detachment, a lack of congruence in our lives."

"Well, that makes sense," Sharon admitted, "but *Dancing Wu Li Masters* was extremely difficult to understand."

Henry agreed and explained that he did not expect her to become a quantum physicist, but rather to have a general understanding of the concept and how it ties in with our spiritual nature.

Sharon sighed and said, "Well, I have read the books and I see what you're talking about. What should I do next?"

"I always recommend that you get on what I call 'The Path.' The Path consists of establishing a daily habit that ties in with your spirituality and also ties in with your right and left brain. It may be a little different at first, but you will find it is an incredible way to support your growth. I would also recommend you read Joseph Jaworski's book, *Synchronicity: The Inner Path to Leadership*. Jaworski talks about enhancing your creativity and about the concept of 'predictable miracles.'"

Sharon asked, " Is Jaworski's inner path 'The Path' you talked about, or just any path, Henry?"

"Good question, Sharon. It is just one path, certainly not The Path. There are many ways to get to The Path," said Henry. "Jaworski's book has worked for me and many others."

"I can hardly wait to learn more. I don't think I have ever experienced a 'predictable miracle,'" Sharon replied.

"I'll give you an overview and we will see," said Henry. "Each morning you should begin with prayer. When you first wake up in the morning and are just conscious that you are awake, your brain has moved from the Delta and Theta states through the Alpha into the Beta. Or perhaps you will be between the Alpha and Beta states. I know you struggled a little with the brain when we were in Cortiza, but I think you will understand these states as you read the book. While you are still in this early consciousness state, you enter into a time of prayer with your Creator. I'm going to make an assumption here that you believe in God.

"Begin with trying to construct a prayer in three parts. First, give thanks to God for all your blessings, for the opportunities that you've had. Fortunately, that won't be difficult for you to do. You have fine health and a supportive mother and father and a wonderful country to live in. Think of everything you can that you are thankful for. Second, enter into prayers of forgiveness. Ask God to forgive you and to help you to actively forgive others, so that when you lay your head down at night, you are not angry with anyone. You should go to sleep in peace, having genuinely forgiven everyone for transgressions of the day and for those hurts of the past. Remember, 'the softest pillow in the world is a clear conscience.'

"Finally, enter into prayers of supplication. You may pray for healing, or for help in reaching goals, or for comfort in times of trial. I always close my prayers of supplication with the caveat, 'not my will but Thy will be done.'"

Sharon sat in silence listening to Henry speak. Prayer had become so foreign in her life, and now she was being asked to pray twice every day! "I'm committed to change," she said, "God has saved me for a purpose; I can do this!"

Henry continued, "This three-part prayer cycle is an excellent way to start every morning. I follow these prayers with a period of meditation. Meditation is a way to shut down the left brain and to give the right brain, the creative, intuitive side, a chance to surface and to be heard. In meditation, you try to stop actively thinking about anything. Your brain Alpha waves are at 10-12 cycles per second, similar to the typical tempo of baroque music. So I meditate to some favorite baroque pieces of Handel, Vivaldi and Boccherini to enhance the Alpha state of my brain.

"Meditation requires a quiet, relaxing environment without distractions and interruptions. I have a favorite chair where I am comfortable. Then I relax with my feet on the floor and turn on Water Music, the first piece on my tape. Next comes the mantra. I can tell from the smile on your face, Sharon, that you think this is ridiculous. And I must admit, most of the people I talk to think that repeating a two-syllable nonsense word is pretty weird. But a mantra is just another technique to quiet the left brain, relax the body and give the right brain a chance.

"Here's how it works. As you breathe in, you say the first syllable; you say the second as you exhale. Focus on your breathing, feeling the air enter and exit your nostrils. Gradually, relax and let the mantra become a substitute for thinking. If thoughts start appearing, gently push them away and return to the soothing, rhythmic mantra. Sometimes this exercise is really difficult to do. But it's not voodoo and it's not silly. It is a proven and effective meditation technique. After awhile, it usually becomes much easier to enter into a meditative state. Your heart pulse slows and your blood pressure will drop. Sometimes people fall asleep and at other times, 15-30 minutes will pass in what may seem like a moment.

"For someone like you, Sharon, with your intelligent, analytic mind, it might not be very easy to let go of your strengths and to meditate. You might want to look into the science and research on meditation, so you will understand the aspects of physiology and biochemistry that accompany the meditative state. But at some point, you just need to take a step into the unknown and experience it for yourself.

"After each meditation session, if your schedule permits, I recommend some vigorous exercise. Get your heartbeat up and your body energized for a busy day. At the very least, it's physically beneficial for you to exercise. But you will find that exercise also enhances the entire prayer-meditation cycle. After your exercise, sit down and review all your written goals.

"Before going to sleep in the evening, go over your written goals again. Your brain waves will move from the Beta state to the Alpha, the Theta and Delta. While you are still in the Beta state, read your goals and then read something spiritual. It could be the Bible or something inspirational and spiritually-based. Then go to sleep. Most people don't know the impact of what we read just before we go to sleep. By reading something inspirational, you will experience a positive impact on your subconscious. You may wake with some new creative thoughts about how to achieve your goals. It will take some doing at first, but stick with the discipline. After awhile this pattern will become a habit. It takes about 21 days to break a habit or to initiate a new one. But once you have incorporated prayer, meditation and spiritual reading into your daily routine, your life will be changed. I look forward to you discovering the changes you are about to experience."

"I'm overwhelmed, Henry. All of this is so new, but it is fascinating. Even the mantra makes sense as a simple technique to help my meditation. But I need help on setting goals. You might be surprised that a finance specialist isn't used to setting personal goals, but I don't even know how to begin."

"I highly recommend you start right away with setting goals for your life. It won't be as hard as you might think. You have set goals all your life, without realizing it. You set goals to finish homework, to graduate from college and to become financially successful. And you have achieved those goals. Now it is time to be more systematic: to look at the five areas of life that I have talked about and to write goals for each area. Remember, those areas are spiritual, physical, relationships, mental and financial. Then you will need to prioritize your goals, so that you can spend your best efforts on your highest goals. And finally, you need to establish short-range and long-range goals. What do you want five years from now? What do you want in two G-curves or three years? Eighteen months? Ninety days? And finally, what are your daily goals? Your goals, of course, will change from time to time, but you have to start some time."

"What in the world is a 'G-curve'?" Sharon asked.

"Actually, I'm not sure where the name came from, but it refers to a psychological experience that occurs over an 18-month period. I've heard colleagues talk about the G-curve, and I've experienced it and observed it for several years. Why does this formula hold true? We don't really know. There may be a better explanation somewhere in the halls of academia, but for now, here is my explanation. When you get highly focused on a major goal over an extended time, there is a strong tendency to make moderate progress in the first six months followed by a plateau for the next 12 months or so. But after 18 months, give or take, people often experience a quantum leap toward achieving the goal. There is tremendous growth in a very short period of time. This pattern occurs so often, that many people who teach techniques of goal-setting build the pattern into the goal-planning process.

"Ironically, many individuals set goals and start down a path toward success, but drop out during the first 12 months. It is rare to find someone with the passion, discipline and persistence to stay focused for 18 months or longer. Yet if people knew about the G-curve, they might be able to keep working long enough to experience the quantum leap breakthrough I've been talking about. I have coached many successful entrepreneurs and recorded this 18-month phenomena for almost everyone. But for every successful entrepreneur, hundreds or thousands give up too soon. And what is really interesting is that a person who stays on a G-curve for 36 months, or for two full G-curve cycles, almost always experiences tremendous growth and success. Fascinating, isn't it?"

"Now everything we talked about at the cabin is beginning to make sense," Sharon replied. "It's a lot of information, but I think

I'm getting it. What do I need to learn next?"

"As long as you've become such an avid reader, I'd like you to read Dr. Herbert Benson's book *The Relaxation Response* before our next meeting. Benson is an MD at Harvard Medical School and has done a lot of research on meditation. There are many kinds and techniques of meditation, so feel free to find one that works for you."

"Henry, how do spirituality and meditation relate to church, to organized religion?"

"I've been waiting for that question, Sharon. Spirituality is an individual matter between you and your Creator. You need to search your heart and soul and belief system to discover what it is that you really believe. It is a seeking process. You will read and listen, pray and study. All a church does is to reinforce these beliefs. A church can put you in touch with people who believe as you do. A church can help you stay steady on a course of inquiry. In the Bible, believers are encouraged to attend church, but it certainly is not a prerequisite for a healthy, spiritual life. You will find people in every church, Sharon, who attend every Sunday and yet lack spirituality. By the same token, there are people who never attend church, who are deeply spiritual."

As they were ready to part, Sharon again hugged her mentor and thanked him fervently for his insights. She vowed that she would get on The Path. She was determined to find an inner peace and to become anchored in her spiritual life.

"I know you will find what you are looking for if you can just maintain your resolve and discipline. My favorite saying is: 'personal discipline leads to personal freedom.' If you develop discipline in your spiritual life, you will find freedom from guilt and anxiety. You will be focused and anchored in your life. Let's talk every few weeks. We will monitor your progress together."

Henry stood, and they said goodbye. Sharon sat back down.

She wanted to reflect for a few moments. As she raised her tea cup to her lips, she allowed her gaze to wander across the water. The restaurant was a favorite of hers; she loved to sit on the flower-covered balcony and watch the boats. Sharon had few friends and hated to eat alone. But this place had always been an exception, a refuge for her loneliness.

Mulling Henry's new plan for her, and his commitment to her progress, she wondered if she would be needing this balcony so much in the future. A smile caught her lips by surprise as she hailed the server for the check.

As Sharon drove home, she let the top down on her convertible. The breeze added to her exultant mood. She was not at all prepared for what she found on her return home. As she opened the heavy wooden door, she saw a white envelope lying on the floor of the foyer. She bent to pick it up, opened the envelope and read the handwritten note inside: "Be alert. Your life is in jeopardy!"

46
Chapter

Gary

Although Gary suffered more physical distress than the others, he returned home with the overriding thought that he had experienced something wonderful. He was neither distraught nor full of anxiety. He was elated to be home safely. Instead of dwelling on the dangers of his trip, his thoughts kept returning to his discussions with Henry. Gary actually felt pretty good about most areas of his life. He had a strong marriage and was close to his two grown sons. He loved his position in human resources and was well respected. If he could only control his weight, he thought wistfully. Most of his life he had borne the jokes and distress. But Henry's assurances had made a lasting impact on him. "I can master this problem," Gary said aloud. With that thought, he picked up the phone and dialed.

Three days later.

"Hi Henry," said Gary, embracing his friend enthusiastically. "I'm really glad that I had a chance to get to know you, even if the circumstances were somewhat unusual. I mean, if we hadn't run for our lives from Guervno, I would never have met you! Thank you so much for agreeing to see me now."

"It's my pleasure," Henry responded. "I really enjoy helping people. What's on your mind?"

"Well, when we were still at the camp waiting to be brought home, you talked about self-esteem. I'd really like to explore that with you. Obviously, I'm very much overweight. I've tried every product and every weight plan. I've got a dozen bottles of chromium picolinate and two dozen diet books. I read recently that about 35 percent of the American people are sufficiently overweight to have a health problem. Nearly 15 percent are morbidly obese, like me," Gary added with a touch of bitterness. "Americans waste two billion dollars a year on fraudulent weight loss products, and I know I'm one of those statistics. For two weeks, I went to bed every night with 'Magic Wrap' around my arms and legs and torso. This miracle invention used batteries to stimulate my muscles and the fat was supposed to melt off as I slept. As you can imagine, it didn't work. It just kept me from sleeping. Then one night, something happened and the wrap overheated. I ended up with terrible burns on my body. So much for 'Miracle Wrap.'

"I've tried everything, but after listening to you, I think there is hope. I'm determined to make this happen. Will you help me?"

"I'd be delighted to work with you, Gary. Let's start with one of my favorite sayings: 'personal discipline leads to personal freedom.' Remember that every discipline affects every other discipline either positively or negatively. If you have the discipline in your life in the areas you want to improve, then you can achieve personal freedom in all areas. Let's take your weight, for example. We both know that excessive weight is a serious health problem. You have already suffered a heart attack. If you can learn the personal discipline necessary to lose excess weight, and more importantly, if you can make the life changes to keep that weight off, imagine the freedom you will experience. With this new freedom, you will enjoy the benefits of improved health, increased energy and enhanced self-esteem.

"Let's start from the standpoint of self-esteem. As I mentioned at the camp, a staggering 90 percent of us have inadequate self-concepts. Yet we have an innate need to feel good about ourselves. There is a terrible conflict in most of us that affects us every day. Secretly, we don't like ourselves. We are not as intelligent or as attractive or as athletic as we want to be. Kids want to be adults. Adults mourn their lost youth. Because we don't have the inner peace that comes from genuinely loving ourselves and being content with who we are, we try to fill the void from the outside. We depend on significant others — parents, siblings, friends, coworkers and also on external signs of success: striving for self-esteem by climbing up the corporate ladder or keeping up with the Joneses. As a result, Americans live with incredible stress. It's no wonder we lead the world in heart disease and strokes.

"But the terrible irony is that external success doesn't build genuine self-esteem. A million dollars in the bank won't do it. Nor a PhD. Nor cosmetic surgery. Self-esteem does not depend on the approval of others. What could be more important than caring for your children? Yet how many women in today's society feel guilty about staying home with the kids? It's pitiful, and it's sad and it's wrong. In my work I see mostly intelligent, well-educated people earning good incomes. And the message I hear from them is that they never quite measure up. Someone with nearly straight As will remember for a lifetime those rare Bs. We believe that we never managed to meet our parents' standards. We never quite measured up to the standard of perfect spouse or loyal friend or successful business person. These negative messages begin when we are surprisingly young. Some pediatricians and child psychologists believe that infants just a few weeks old can start perceiving disapproval of their parents. And these potentially damaging perceptions are reinforced throughout our lives and into adulthood. Statistically, by the time you are eight years old, 80 percent of your self-esteem is already determined. As a result, most of us live out a script that was written for us by others.

"By middle school, we are experts in criticism. Cruelty abounds for the kid with a speech impediment, a learning disability or a weight problem. We've all heard the taunts and the nicknames. But it's not only these kids who suffer. We all try desperately to belong, to be part of some crowd, to be normal and to measure up to the mysterious standards of the day. Consequently, we nearly lose our ability to truly become ourselves and to celebrate our individuality.

"O.K., that's the basic concept. Now let me generalize a bit for the purpose of illustration. There are three main categories of people in terms of concepts of self-worth. The first category, say 40 percent, is people who have fundamentally negative self-esteem, negative about themselves and about life in general. They see the proverbial glass as half-empty at best. Their negative self-esteem moves them to constantly criticize others. Whatever worth they find in themselves is achieved at the expense of attacking others.

"The second category, perhaps another 40 percent, consists of those who are much more positive about the world around them. They have heroes and role models to emulate, and they strive to be more like those they admire and respect. But their self-esteem is still lacking. They still do not set their goals based on self-analysis, but rather strive to be like someone else — thinner, more attractive, more athletic, richer, more successful than themselves.

"Finally there are those who have adequate self-esteem, or

who are moving toward what Carl Rogers and Abraham Maslow call 'self-fulfillment' or 'self-actualization.' People in this group are learning to make choices based on their internal needs and desires. They are learning to set and achieve personal goals without reliance on the approval and permission of others. They tend to pursue a hobby or a profession because of a deep love or passion. They work for goals and celebrate the pursuit. They are remarkably resilient and seldom get discouraged if they fall short of a goal. Their self-esteem is intact, even in failure. And, not surprisingly, self-actualized people tend to be conspicuous achievers.

"I think it is absolutely fascinating to study those who are lowest on the self-esteem continuum. The bottom 5 percent are so profoundly negative that they typically turn to drugs and alcohol to shore themselves up against a sense of inadequacy. Most should be institutionalized or receiving professional care. Some are dangerous to themselves and to others. Some are suicidal, ready to commit the ultimate act of despair and despondency.

"Just above this bottom 5 percent of social dropouts is another 5 percent of people who are deeply troubled, but whose behaviors are radically different. Instead of hiding from society through drugs or alcohol, this group manifests completely different behavior. They are egomaniacs, driven to success by a compulsive need to feel O.K. Even though they suffer from a deep sense of inadequacy, they may be among the most successful achievers and leaders. Quite a few military leaders can serve as classic examples. Studies often cite Adolph Hitler as another. Given the right channel for their obsessive behavior, this group of people can accomplish things. Many go into highly-extroverted professions like sales or politics, sports or acting. They become skilled speakers and adept at presenting themselves in the very best light. These people must succeed to feed their egos, and their drive often propels them to conspicuous achievement.

"Those who are stimulated by energy and power typify this group. But don't expect close personal friendships to develop.

These people are driven by their need to succeed and they can be ruthlessly Machiavellian, stepping over friends and business associates to reach the brass ring of success. While they seem powerful and successful, they also tend to be highly vulnerable. They cannot stand failure, often living on the edge of despair. They enjoy the thrill of victory with each success; but after the blush fades, they need another, greater success. In essence they are addicted to the excitement of conquest. Perhaps it is not surprising then, that many slip into other forms of addiction, including the deep depression of drug and alcohol dependency, but they still feel compelled to enjoy the limelight. They may experience huge mood swings, being the life of the party one day and subject to fits of rage and depression the next. They often spend money irresponsibly and need constant financial rewards to fuel their lifestyle. But this dangerous and compulsive path often leads to financial and emotional ruin, so like the first group, these people are at high risk for suicide.

"Now you can see why I spend so much time talking about self-esteem. It takes a lot of hard work to get out of the patterns we learned as children. Remember I said that it takes three things to make a major change in an individual's self-worth. First, it takes knowledge. In the next weeks, I will suggest some books to read and we will look in depth at the factors that influenced the development of your self-concept. Next, you need a significant emotional experience. Finally, of course, you need to take action to change your self-worth. Taking action is greatly enhanced after experiencing a significant emotional experience or SEE."

"I studied significant emotional experiences in college," said Gary, "but I would like for you to describe them in your own words."

"O.K., you realize that you just had one with Guervno. You thought you were going to die. You started making peace with your Creator. It was a very traumatic experience for you and for your friends. You all resolved to make some changes in your lives should you somehow be rescued from your fate. Some of you tried to make bargains with God. Now you want to make some changes in your life. This is the optimum time to move ahead with those changes. But significant emotional experiences don't have to be as dramatic as a brush with death. It could be a divorce or a serious illness of your child; it could be bankruptcy or moving to a new city to accept a new job. For many people with weight challenges, a picture of themselves will trigger a SEE. It could even be going to a certain seminar or a movie or reading a particular book. Many successful entrepreneurs can cite a moment in their lives when some event crystallized years of thoughts and dreams and aspirations.

"The key is that after some significant experience, you make a commitment to action, to changing your life. Finally you say with conviction: 'I'm not going to stay in this job any more. I'm going to work on my marriage. I'm going to permanently lose weight and become a healthier person.' The important thing is that a significant emotional experience is followed by action. I call the pattern 'K SEE A,' or Knowledge, Significant Emotional Experience and Action.

"You have just had a dramatic significant emotional experience. And you are soaking up knowledge like a sponge. This is a very exciting crossroad in your life and I'm honored to be a part of it. Now it is a matter of following through with the action necessary to change your behavior. You've talked about how many times you have begun a plan or program to lose weight, and then given up after some success. We have to conquer that cycle of failure. Let's start with a few excellent resources that I know will be helpful. The first is Jack Canfield's tape series, *How to Build High Self-Esteem*. It is excellent for all ages. Next, I'd recommend a book by Nathaniel Branden, *The Six Pillars of Self-Esteem*. Finally, if you want to get a little deeper into the subject of self-concept, I'd recommend a classic called *Psycho-Cybernetics* by Maxwell Maltz. After you have listened to the tapes and read the books, let's get together again, probe a little deeper and begin planning a course of action."

"This is great!" Gary enthused. "Those terrible days at Guervno's camp and then our trek through the jungle were the worst days of my life. I was sure my heart was going to give out and I'd die in the jungle. But Nietzsche once said: 'whatever does not destroy us makes us stronger.' I feel stronger and more confident than I can ever remember. I'm going to change my life. And guess what? I lost eight pounds in my ordeal, and so far, I haven't gained those pounds back. It's a start."

"It's a great start, Gary, and congratulations. In the next couple of days, I want you to take a test called the 'Tennessee Self-Concept Scale.' I'll give you a copy so you can take the test at home at your leisure. Then send the test in to the address on the envelope to be computer scored. After you receive the computer printout, I strongly urge you to work with a professional counselor who understands this test. He or she can interpret the results much better than I can. You may want to wait to take the test until you've digested all the material I've suggested for you. That's up to you."

"This is all so fascinating, Henry; thank you so much. I will get right to those tapes and books, and I'm already looking forward to our next meeting."

"Before you go," said Henry, "let's talk a little about your weight and about discipline or will power. You have told me how hard it has been to lose weight and keep it off. That is such a familiar pattern. Losing weight can be a difficult and discouraging process. It doesn't feel good to diet. It is uncomfortable to be hungry. Many people get headaches or feel exhausted or even get ill as they go through the trauma of losing weight. Most people lose weight, then gain it back, then lose it again in a constant yo-yo process that actually begins to damage muscle tissue. Dieting can be a very dangerous process without the watchful eye and advice of a physician. And weight loss medications can be even more harmful.

"A lot of companies make money selling weight loss products and ideas. And look at all the free advertising they are getting! A few months ago I spent some time at a large bookstore and looked at magazines. There were 16 so-called women's magazines, and every one had something about weight loss on the front cover. Every one! Then there are the weight and fitness magazines, the health and holistic medicine magazines, and the tabloid papers announcing breakthrough weight loss secrets. Then look at the books, dozens and dozens of them. Two are on the best-seller list. Americans seem obsessed by weight loss.

"But you know something? Weight loss is only a small part of the problem. The bigger issue is self-concept. For most people, an improved self-concept and personal discipline would put the weight loss folks out of business. Sensible nutrition and a discipline of daily exercise would take care of most obesity. But most people seem to lack the discipline. They are willing to starve themselves for a few days, or to drink gallons of water for a few more, but they probably do themselves much more harm than good as they continually get on the wagon and fall off again.

"I'm really looking forward to hearing about your progress for the next 30 days. These days will be important, because they will take you past the 21-day habit-breaking barrier. I really think you are going to make it, Gary. I don't just mean that you are going to lose weight. I mean that you are going to change your life. You will lose the weight and keep it off. You will be successful because you will be changed inside, in your essential self-concept. The first thing I want you to do is to get a very thorough physical exam. Have your doctor check your heart. Do another treadmill test and get all the blood workups. As soon as your doctor approves your regimen, I want you to commit to 30 minutes of vigorous exercise every day. Whatever you do, don't give up. You can swim or jog or walk or bicycle, or climb stairs, but do that 30 minutes every day. Then eat sensibly. You know what to eat; you've probably read every nutrition book on the shelves. You know the drill: lots of fruits and vegetables and complex carbohydrates. Stay away from white bread and sugar and fats. Drink lots of water and count the calories.

"Those old habits may torment you for awhile. You may want to get up at night and eat a quart of ice cream. You may get anxiety attacks and crave food. That's when you should drink a pint of water and go out for another walk. Take control of your life. And watch the pounds start melting. You might want to join a fitness center, one that has a fitness counselor who can encourage you and give you a variety of exercises. You know that on average, people drop out after 18 days. Eighteen days! Just before they have a chance to incorporate a new habit! Try to make a new friend who will exercise with you, and you can encourage each other. But make a commitment, and refuse to quit.

"Once exercise and a sensible nutrition plan are established, start setting some specific short-range and long-range goals. Be sure these goals can be measured and achieved. They might include weight loss, distance and duration goals, cholesterol levels, blood pressure measurements or the time it takes you to walk a mile. Make charts and keep your records. We can review your progress once a week over the phone and then see each other once a month, bringing in everything for us to review. You need to put some time into learning about health and weight loss. I would recommend you read *Make the Connection* by Bob Greene and Oprah Winfrey. Oprah has been very open about her personal struggle with weight. She has certainly proven to be a good role model when it comes to permanent change versus a 'quick fix.'"

"I'm going to do it," Gary said. "Not because you told me to, but because it is what I want and need to do. I've made this promise 100 times before, but this time things are different. I can't explain it, but I'm committed. Maybe it has something to do with my significant emotional experience. Maybe it is having a few new friends I can count on to help encourage me until I'm strong enough to do this completely on my own. But whatever it is, I'm looking forward to seeing you in a month. You will be able to see the difference."

"I'm sure I will," responded Henry with a quiet confidence.

"You remind me of another person I counseled a few years ago. He lost 110 pounds, and has kept off that weight for years. His methods were simple. He used to eat six or eight cheeseburgers at one sitting. He still eats a cheeseburger once in awhile, but only one. He has one beer a week instead of a couple of six-packs a day. He savors the cheeseburger and the beer, but limits his indulgences. He has stopped smoking and walks an hour every day. Simple things, but what a profound difference they have made! I really think you are going to succeed, Gary, and I am delighted to hear that you are not trying to please me, but to meet your personal goals. Your self-esteem has already taken a quantum leap!

"One more thought on weight loss, Gary. Some people lose weight easier than others. Genetics plays a part. So does our biochemistry, our metabolism and even our age. But the biggest factor is lifestyle. Increase your physical activity and decrease your calories and you will lose weight. But that doesn't mean to run a marathon and starve yourself. You are in this for the long run, changing your lifestyle, literally changing your habits, for the rest of your life. And I strongly recommend that you let science help you. A nutritionist can recommend a vitamin/mineral supplement. There are supplements proven safe and effective in accelerating the metabolism and fat loss. But please be sure a qualified doctor oversees your weight loss program. You will need to begin with a complete physical.

"My last piece of advice is to be disciplined, but also to use moderation. Research tells us that a glass of red wine a day is healthy and actually promotes weight loss. Yet I see alcohol abuse every day. The same is true of weight loss programs. Be patient and remember my motto: 'personal discipline leads to personal freedom.' The next time we meet, I will have more material for you to read. I'm a big fan of Dr. Kenneth Cooper of the Cooper Clinic in Dallas; he has a number of excellent books. You might want to start with *Advanced Nutritional Therapies*. But you've got plenty to work on for now, so get started on your self-esteem assignments and a sensible program of diet and exercise. Until we get together again, I wish you the best of luck."

"Thanks a million, Henry. I'm on my way, I'm sure of it."

When Gary got home, carrying a new bottle of high-potency vitamins and minerals, he smiled with pride. He knew he was embarking on a new, permanent lifestyle. This time he would follow through with his commitment. As he unlocked the door, he heard the phone ringing. Rushing in, he picked up the phone and said, "Hello."

A heavy, gravely voice finally broke the silence. "Is this Gary Wilson?"

"Yes, I'm Gary Wilson." There was a pause. Gary was waiting for the sales pitch for a magazine subscription or vinyl siding. Breaking the silence, Gary proffered, "May I help you?"

There was a low, malicious chuckle interrupted by the disconnection as the caller hung up. Gary stood looking at the receiver for several seconds before he slowly cradled it. His fingers lingered on it as an uneasy feeling crept into his stomach.

Chapter 47

Kevin

Kevin seemed less affected by the Cortiza experience than his colleagues. He had been terrified with the others, but somehow managed to put those events behind him. There was one bright light in that his wife had come to the airport. Maybe there was hope. He wanted to learn more about himself, especially his inability to maintain relationships; but he lacked the commitment to change and the enthusiasm the others had expressed for meeting with Henry and continuing their discussions. He thought about his wife and his three boys. He knew the signs: his marriage was failing. Worse yet, his boys were almost strangers. I suppose a visit to Henry couldn't hurt, he thought. So, expecting little, Kevin called.

He was pleasantly surprised and pleased when Henry agreed to meet and work with him. But Henry insisted on Kevin's commitment to change his life, particularly regarding relationships. Kevin didn't much care for the prerequisite, but agreed to meet with Henry anyway. He admitted that he was curious to explore his problems, despite his reluctance to really open up and share his personal feelings. But he was well aware of his inability to maintain good relationships. So he sought Henry's advice with mixed emotions. Kevin would have to drive over three hours to meet with Henry. Henry knew that even if it was only on a sub-conscious level, Kevin really wanted to change.

When they met, Henry started with pointed questions: "Kevin, what is it that you want out of life? What is important to you?"

Kevin was slow to answer, irritated by the bold intrusion into his personal thoughts and feelings. Yet there was something about Henry that inspired trust. In fact, Kevin began to realize that he really wanted to talk to this extraordinary man. "Well," he began awkwardly, "my life is pretty good. I have no major com-plaints." For some reason, Kevin suddenly felt ashamed. He was putting on the same little act he put on with everyone. He started over. "It's just that I can't seem to establish relationships. Everything else seems to come so easily for me. I'm not sure why, but after Cortiza I feel as if I might have reached a teach-able moment in my life. At the same time, it wasn't easy for me to come here. I don't know if I am ready or able to make the kind of commitment you are asking of me. In fact, I'm afraid you are going to 'fire' me as a client who just isn't ready for you." Kevin laughed awkwardly and was astonished to discover tears welling up in his eyes.

"Thanks for your honesty, Kevin," Henry said in a voice as warm and welcome as fresh baked bread. In that moment, Kevin felt a surge of kinship with his mentor. Just as suddenly, Henry dove into his subject with a sense of urgent purpose: "Let's start with some statistics. In this country, 52 percent of all marriages end in divorce. That's not a very good record, and the success rate for second marriages is even lower. You might think that people would learn from their mistakes and enter second marriages older and wiser. But the numbers don't bear that out. People tend to make the same mistakes the second and third time around. They carry the same baggage into new marriages. It is essential that we understand the dynamics of our relationships and then make changes, or we are likely to repeat our failures.

"As I said in our camp talks in Cortiza and as I say to everyone I counsel, there are three steps to changing the patterns in our lives. The first is knowledge. The second is having a significant emotional experience, something that forces us out of our daily patterns and habits. And the final step is taking action, making a commitment to changing our lives so that we can more effectively reach our goals.

"So if we start working together, I am going to help you complete these steps. First, I'm going to recommend some excellent books on relationships to stimulate your thinking and increase your knowledge. You've already been through your significant emotional experience, and I'm sure that is why you feel somewhat ready to explore new options in your life. You mentioned that this might be a 'teachable moment' for you. That is a very perceptive statement and very accurate. Finally, however, you have to do some work. You have to make a commitment to a plan of action to change. If you are not willing to act in your own behalf, then you are almost certain to continue the habits that have led to two failed marriages and another one at risk.

"Kevin, what most people do after a failed marriage is to blame the other person. To begin to change it is necessary to accept responsibility for your role in the breakup. Without a desire to change, and the realization that you are partially responsible, you will keep walking the same well-worn path. Let's start with knowledge. What have you read? What kind of seminars have you attended that have helped you to build wonderful, solid, intimate relationships?"

Kevin bowed his head and admitted, "I guess I've never studied relationships."

Henry smiled. "In that case, you are in for some great reading. First, get Gary Smalley's book, *Making Love Last Forever*. And you must read Erich Fromm's absolute classic, *The Art of Loving*. I know you are very intelligent and a quick study, Kevin, but these books are more than facts and data. Try to read them slowly and think about the concepts. In recent years, Dr. John Gray has made great strides in helping people understand many of the reasons relationships fail. Go to your local book store and ask for his Mars and Venus series. I'm sure you will find one of his books relevant to your personal experience. Second, Kevin, is your self-esteem. Learn to like yourself. It may be a long journey to feeling really good about yourself, but if you really want to grow, if you really want to change your life, you need to start down the path of improving your self-esteem. Next time we meet I will give you a list of books on that topic.

"Please don't be offended, Kevin, but I've noticed that you are impatient with others, especially when they seem illogical. You have very little regard for the feelings, the intuitions and the fears of others. There is a whole world of emotion out there that you have largely ignored. Friendship, intimacy, the love that is shared by parents and their children: these transcend the limited realms of logic. I think you have to learn how to love and how to be loved. Let me know what thoughts are inspired by Smalley's book. In fact, I think working on your self-esteem is the single most important thing you can do at this point." Henry suggested a couple of resources in self-esteem that he had recently given to Gary.

Kevin sat in silence for a moment and then said, "Henry, I'm not sure what I'm committing to, but I promise to give this journey a try. I do love my children, although I'm not sure if they have any feelings left for me. And I realize my third marriage may crumble if I don't do some things differently. I really don't want to become a three-time loser. And I don't want to lose my children."

190

Henry smiled again and put a hand on Kevin's shoulder. "You know, Kevin, I almost told you that I wasn't ready to spend time with you. But I was wrong. With those sparks of insight, I think you can change. In fact, I think you can save your marriage and discover something very exciting in the process. I genuinely wish you luck. Let's meet again in a couple of weeks and really discuss those books and tapes I recommended."

Kevin left feeling better than he had for years. He had decided to fight for his marriage and to really work toward changing. Maybe it took a near-death experience to shake him out of his cocoon. When he left the restaurant and walked to the parking garage, he found a note on his windshield. With difficulty, he made out the scrawled handwriting on the crumpled note: "You have not escaped!"

48 *Chapter*

Michelle

Michelle arrived home from her adventure so confused that she found it difficult to sort out her feelings. She was depressed and frightened, finding it nearly impossible to focus on her work. Her husband and her children had been great, but she felt she had lost herself. Despite her lack of a college degree, she had quickly risen to prominence as a computer whiz. But her experiences in Cortiza made her realize how one-dimensional she was. She wanted to expand her horizons, to learn about history and literature and especially about countries like Cortiza. Why was she no longer content to be the very best in her field? She was respected for her ability and well-paid, but she wanted more. She began thinking about the spiral staircase.

I need to talk to Henry, she thought. I'm sure he can help me sort through this mess. I just want to find the complete me — the butterfly that is ready to emerge. At least I hope there is a butterfly inside me. I just wish I hadn't lost that journal. I guess Henry can make me another one.

Henry willingly agreed to meet with Michelle as he had with the other Cortiza team members. He had settled into a pattern of getting together at comfortable, neutral spots like restaurants and coffee houses. Michelle had to fly in so Henry agreed to meet at one of the restaurants at the airport. They met for lunch; and typical of Henry's direct style, they were soon talking about Michelle's concerns.

"I've been thinking about all the things that have happened to us in the last few weeks. I realize that my life has been so narrowly focused on programming and troubleshooting that I've missed out on a whole big world. I want to know more, to grow and learn and maybe even discover that I'm good at other things. I've never listened to classical music. Maybe I'll hate it. But at least then I'll know that I hate it."

Henry couldn't resist a chuckle. He liked this personable woman who had so few pretenses.

"Sure, I'm successful at what I do. And I really enjoy it. But it's the only thing I've ever done. I'm in my 40s and I'm just beginning to realize that computers are the only things I know. I'm a geek, a computer nerd. Maybe I don't look like the stereotype, but it's true."

"Michelle," Henry said, "you are not alone in feeling that you don't fit in or that life is somehow passing you by. America has a literacy rate of 97 percent, but 76 percent of the adult population did not read a book last year. You said in Cortiza that you had not read a book in almost five years. Is that true?"

"Yes," answered Michelle, "other than what I have to read for work. I just don't read anything else."

"Think about it this way, Michelle. There really isn't much difference between an illiterate person and one who just doesn't read."

"Well I guess that's probably true, but most of the people I know don't seem to read much — not even magazines or the newspaper."

"Unfortunately, you are right," Henry agreed. "Did you know that only 3 percent of Americans have library cards? Interestingly, that is about the same percentage of people who have written down their goals. Do you happen to know what your reading level is? The average adult reads about 300 words a minute at the sixth grade level. How about you?"

"Well, I'm not a speed reader by any stretch of the imagination, and I do get bored reading books and magazines outside my field; so I have plenty of room to improve there. I'm really not interested in reading novels; they've always seemed like a waste of time to me. But I do want to learn," she added hastily, afraid she might have offended her advisor.

"You'd be surprised how much you can learn from a good piece of fiction, Michelle," Henry said gently. "But for now, let's take the path of least resistance. Let's get you on a speed-reading program and select the kinds of information you are most interested in exploring. It is not difficult to get your reading up to 1,000 words per minute with a self-taught speed-reading course. Interestingly, as you learn to read faster, your comprehension increases, because there is less chance of getting bored with the material. I can recommend two or three very good speed-reading courses.

"Next, get the Jim Rohn tape series, *Challenge to Succeed in the 90's*. Listen to these tapes and start thinking about what you can do to discover your talents and potential. I'm not suggesting that you stop your interest in computers. You are very gifted and also have the ability to explain computer concepts to others. But

I think you will find Rohn very interesting. He is a master word-smith; just concentrate on his ideas that appeal to you and we will talk about those next time we meet. Also, I'd strongly recommend that you keep writing in your journal."

"Henry, I forgot to bring the journal I started in Cortiza. Could you replace the exercises on priorities and the other worksheets?"

"Of course," said Henry, "I believe most of the team left them behind when we ran for the helicopter.

"Go out and purchase a new one and I'll replace the work-sheets. One of the fascinating things you will observe as you keep a journal is your personal growth. There are no rules to a journal. Just write your feelings and thoughts and ideas. Don't bother with writing everything you do during the day from brushing your teeth to weeding the garden. Instead, make this a journal of inquiry and discovery, your personal and totally private record of thoughts and feelings. Assume that everything in your journal is, and always will be, totally private. That doesn't mean that you can't share something that you decide you want to share. But no one has a right to ask you to break that precious bond of safety and privacy. I will never ask you to share anything that is there. You need to be comfortable about writing anything and everything, without worrying about what is proper, or whether you spelled a word correctly, or if your penmanship is attractive enough.

"I *do* recommend that you write on a wide variety of subjects. Record your thoughts from books you read. Write about the new things you have learned. I encourage you to read and read and read, whatever sustains your interest. You would like Napoleon Hill's *Think and Grow Rich*. It's a classic in its field and one that will stimulate conversation when we meet again. And you might want to tackle Ayn Rand's *Atlas Shrugged*, a book I consider to be one of the most incredible ever written. In a recent survey, 70 percent of a group of CEOs identified this book to be the most influential book in their lives after the Bible. I'd also like you to read *Dare to Win*, and *The Aladdin Factor* by Mark Victor Hansen. I look forward to meeting with you and discussing the provocative ideas in these books. I wish you all the luck in the world."

Michelle felt much more at peace after her talk with Henry. She was grateful that the man seated next to her on the plane fell asleep almost immediately and made no small talk. When the flight attendant came by, Michelle even declined the food so she could relax and enjoy the luxury of quiet thinking. When the plane landed she was ready to walk back into her present life.

It was late when she arrived at her home. The windows were dark. She knew she had missed putting her children to bed. She loved the smell of their freshly washed little bodies, the patter of bare feet in the long hallway, and the hugs and cuddling at bedtime. She liked to read and tell them stories. Now she had more advanced reading to do. She would wake her husband, she decided. She had much to tell him!

Her hand was eagerly reaching for the door when she saw the note: "YOU WILL PAY." She tore it off, clutching it to her breast in fear. She was relieved that her sleeping family had not seen the ominous threat, even as her concern for them grew.

Garrett

After Garrett returned from Cortiza, he spent a considerable number of hours reviewing his life. By most standards he was successful. He was a respected attorney held in high regard by the business community. He had held several responsible positions in his local church. He was a strong leader who inspired confidence in others with his resonant voice and the courage of his convictions. He had a beautiful new wife who was completely devoted to him and he certainly had proved himself of great value in Cortiza, taking charge of the group. Yet, he thought, what do I have to show for my life? I have no money in the bank, no investments, no retirement. If I see the latest sports car, I just have to have it, even though I'm still paying for the one I've got. How can I get my life in order?

With those thoughts, Garrett made an appointment to meet Henry in a quaint seafood restaurant in his home town. Henry was going to be in town for another meeting and agreed to see Garrett while he was there. They found a private table away from the noise and Garrett plunged right in. "I make a very good living, Henry. But I spend to the very edge of what I earn. If I were to get sick or injured for a few months, I'd lose everything. I've got to get control of my financial life."

"Well, let me ask you some questions, Garrett. Have you set any financial goals? Have you written them down?"

Garrett sighed and said, "I know I should have written goals and a plan for monitoring my progress, but I've always relied on my income to keep me going. I can see that I need to start a systematic plan."

"You are exactly right, Garrett. You need to write down what you want to accomplish and a plan to achieve those goals. Obviously, you are going to have to make some changes in your lifestyle. But you have the benefits of both a very good income and also time to put your financial house in order. It's really a matter of principles, universal truths. If you throw a ball up, it comes down at a predictable trajectory and rate of speed. If you invest a certain sum at a certain rate of interest over a given time, you can calculate your returns.

"I have always believed," Henry continued, "that money is attracted rather than pursued. If you fill the needs of enough people, then your financial needs will be met. Most people, 93 percent, trade their time for money. They spend so many hours and weeks and years at a job in return for compensation. About 3 percent trade money for money, earning their incomes through investments. And finally, about 3 to 4 percent of people trade other people's time and money for money. If you want to be wealthy, you need to move to that last category."

"I'm not sure what you mean," said Garrett.

"Well, let's say you write a bestselling book. You do initially invest the time to write the book. But once the book starts to sell, you are trading other people's time and money for money. As the book gets to the marketplace, clerks sell it and eventually you get a check. Some people have written hit songs in 20 or 30 minutes and profited from those songs for a lifetime. In fact, I once met the guy who wrote 'Listen to the Rhythm of the Falling Rain.' He was on watch in the Navy one night and wrote the song out there in the middle of the ocean. It was raining and he had nothing to do, so he took out a pen and wrote the song. He sent it to Ricky Nelson and it became a hit, recorded by umpteen artists.

"What you have to do is to find a vehicle that you can either build on your own, or that you can buy from someone else, that generates income from other people's time and money. That is basically how franchises work. At the beginning, you trade your time to build a machine. But that machine can grow into a powerful empire with you earning your money from hundreds or thousands of people investing their time and money. It is a powerful and proven concept worthy of careful consideration.

"I also suggest you read *The Four Laws of Debt Free Prosperity* by Blaine Harris and Charles Coonradt. I'll quickly summarize their four laws:

- Track where every penny goes.

- Set targets or goals.

- Live on less than you earn while getting out of debt and investing in appreciating assets.

- Train and prepare.

"I compress the four principles into the four Ts: track, target, trim and train. It's pretty basic and common sense stuff, but most people don't follow these principles."

"Anything else, Henry?"

"When you're ready to begin investing, I strongly recommend you start with a fee-only financial planner. Instead of making commissions by buying and selling investments, he or she will manage your portfolio for an annual fee. Your planner can recommend many no-load investments and insurance policies. I also recommend you read a fascinating book called *Investment Biker* by Jim Rogers. I won't spoil it by telling you what it is about, but I think you'll love it. Other books I think you should read are *Hardcastle's Money Talk*, David Chilton's *The Wealthy Barber*, and Tod Barnhart's *The Five Rituals of Wealth*. I know this is a lot of reading, but you can't go wrong with these great books. Make reading them a priority; then let's get together to discuss them."

Garrett wrote down the book titles and agreed to get started right away. In fact, he could hardly wait. But as he left the restaurant, his enthusiasm was dimmed by a premonition that something was amiss. He tried to brush the nagging feeling aside, but his uneasiness increased. Maybe I'm just exhausted from my ordeal in Cortiza, he thought. Only time would tell.

50
Chapter

In Search of the Summit

During the next few months, Henry held weekly calls with each member of the team. And Henry was gratified that the team members called each other once in awhile too. Gradually, one by one, they each began living on a whole new level of awareness. They were on The Path. Much of Henry's time was devoted to the growth of his new students. They were eight months into their commitments to change, and all of them had reached plateaus. Henry knew that this was a difficult time. Gary had stopped losing weight, but to his credit, showed no signs of giving up. Something in the Cortiza experience had given him a deep sense of determination. Worried that the others might drift away from their goals, Henry named each team member during his daily meditation. Would they make it to see the power of the G-curve?

Chapter

51

Eighteen Months After Escape

O n the same auspicious day early in October, messengers delivered a personal engraved invitation to each member of "Team El Frando" and their families. Henry wanted to gather the group together one full G-curve after Cortiza.

Sharon was sitting at her desk at work, when a uniformed messenger presented her with a beautiful bouquet of flowers. Her invitation was attached to the enclosed card. Gary was working out at his local health club, when his invitation arrived. A man dressed in a black tuxedo approached Gary as he rounded the jogging track. Michelle received hers as she was retrieving the mail from her ivy-covered mailbox. It was one of the local delivery services known for their punctuality.

The invitations were engraved on ivory rag linen paper. The copy read, "In life we have but one birth and one death. You will only be remembered for the lives of the people you have touched in between. You are counted among the few who have searched for the true meaning of life. I am honored to call you friend. Please join me in a special celebration of our first G-curve. Families, of course, are welcome. RSVP."

On the bottom of the invitation it listed the time, date and location. They were simply signed, "Henry."

The team couldn't wait to see everyone again.

Chapter

52

The Celebration

M ichelle gasped when she saw Gary. He looked great! "I broke the 200-pound barrier two weeks ago," he said beaming. "I'm six feet two and weigh 198 pounds. It's the lightest I've been since high school!"

"It's not just the weight, Gary," Michelle said. "I mean, you look really good, tan and athletic. And you look so much younger!"

Gary laughed. "I do feel terrific. I started golfing and now I'm a fanatic. I carry my bags and walk every course. If they require golf carts, I won't play the course. I figure in a round of golf, I probably walk five miles. I'm still not very good but I have a 16 handicap and I just shot my first round under 90. But you know what is even better? I'm golfing with my two boys. It is so much fun!"

"I just can't get over it," Michelle continued. "It's practically a miracle. And look at Kevin! He has a group of people around him. That introvert is actually talking to people and laughing. Better yet, they are laughing with him! And who is the beautiful woman on his arm?"

"That's his wife. The one who was going to leave him."

Michelle just shook her head in delighted wonder.

"So what are you up to?" Gary asked. "Still the computer whiz kid?"

"Yeah," Michelle said. "But I've got a new hobby. You'll never guess. I've started reading mysteries. At first Henry got me reading history and science and philosophy. I told him I didn't want to have anything to do with fiction. Then he suggested I read Poe's short story, 'The Purloined Letter.' And I got hooked. I really like Agatha Christie and Ngaio Marsh, but my favorite sleuth is Sherlock Holmes. I just bought an annotated edition of Conan Doyle and I spend more time reading the footnotes than the text! The funny thing is that I've always enjoyed my job. But now I like it better than ever. I was always afraid that if I started learning other things, I'd become dissatisfied with my work. But it has been just the opposite. I know that for some reason I have a talent with computers, and I am lucky to have discovered that and to have a great job that lets me use that talent. At the same time, I'm finding there is a great big world out there that's fascinating and fun!"

"That is wonderful, Michelle," Gary said sincerely. "You have obviously come a long way. From the look of it, I guess we all have. Let's continue this talk at dinner. But in the meantime, I've just got to see what Kevin is up to."

As soon as Kevin noticed his colleagues, he called out, "Michelle, Gary! It's great to see you. Come over here and meet my wife."

On a sofa near one end of the room, Garrett sat with Henry talking quietly. "I can't thank you enough, Henry. You started out as our counsellor and mentor coach, but you have become a close friend to all of us. My life is so much better now that I have goals and a plan for financial security. The best part is that I no longer have the financial anxiety. I still don't have a fortune, but I am on a path of responsible investments. Would you believe it, I'm driving a Ford Taurus! It's not sexy, but it is practical. And the insurance premium is less than 10 percent of what I was paying on the BMW. An exotic sports car is still in my goals. But it's going to take about three more years for me to accomplish higher priorities."

"You know, Garrett, it's remarkable that all five of you have stayed in touch and maintained your friendships. Not only that, all five of you have made dramatic progress in achieving your goals. I especially wanted all of you to meet together at this time. Remember when I talked about the 'G-curve?' Did you realize that before you received your invitation that it had been about 18 months since all of you started setting goals and systematically working toward them? It is no coincidence that you have made such remarkable progress. Gary, for example, lost weight and then reached a plateau. But he didn't get discouraged, and his discipline pushed him to increase his exercise. He began losing weight and then got to another, even more stubborn plateau. But he persisted with confidence and determination. And last month he lost 6 pounds, dropping below his goal of 200 pounds. There is something almost magical about setting goals and working toward them. I can't tell you how many times I have seen people reach a goal right before a deadline."

"Can I interrupt?" asked Sharon.

"Please join us," Garrett said as he and Henry stood and took turns hugging her.

"Thank you, dear friends," said Sharon. "This was a wonderful idea, Henry. And I'm so glad everyone made it."

"There is something different about you, Sharon," said Garrett, "but I can't tell you what it is. This may sound funny, but I think you look more relaxed. Yes, that's part of it. I remember that you always talked rapidly. We slow-talking Southerners notice things like that. In fact, you just seem, well, content."

"What a nice thing to say," Sharon responded laughing. "And very perceptive of you. For the first time in my life I feel at peace. Or at least I'm learning to be at peace. Henry has coached me through some very hard times, but just in the last two months, meditation has really become a meaningful part of my life. So many times I thought about giving up. There were days when I just felt foolish trying to repeat my mantra and letting my creative side have a chance to express itself. But I think I've passed through some kind of barrier. 'I've got miles to go before I sleep,' of course, and I have so much to learn. But I'm on The Path if you know what I mean," she said smiling.

"You know something, Sharon?" Garrett said. "You are yet one more proof that there is something to this 'G-curve' that Henry talks about. In fact, everyone I've talked to seems to have made some kind of quantum leap of progress in the past few weeks."

"Yes," said Sharon, "something truly has happened to us. But there was a time when I thought Guervno had come back to get us. I got this, well, vague anonymous threat. It was terrifying."

Each team member suddenly started talking about their own calls, notes, and threats. For some reason, none had gone to the police. In fact, not one of them had even talked to another team member about this disturbing mystery. Where was Guervno? He must somehow be behind all of this. Was he coming to get them? Why had the threats stopped? They each described what had happened after their first meeting with Henry.

"It must have been the journals that some of you left behind," said Henry. "I know Michelle had each of your names and addresses in her journal. Guervno must have sent someone to the States to threaten you. But that was more than a year ago. I'm sure the danger, if there ever was a danger, must have passed."

The conversation continued until someone announced that dinner was served. Everyone gathered around the banquet table in a private room. All the chairs but one were occupied. "Is someone missing?" Michelle asked, noting that salads had been placed at every setting.

"Yes," answered Henry, "there *is* one person missing. Actually, he is a surprise guest. Would anyone like to make a guess?"

"I hope it's not Guervno!" Kevin exclaimed.

The group broke out in a riot of laughter and groans.

"No, I think you'll agree our guest is somewhat more welcome than Guervno. Ladies and gentlemen," Henry announced with a flair, "may I present my closest friend, my brother . . . Duke Milligan."

The group watched in stunned silence as Duke entered the room smiling. "Don't all applaud at once," he said, breaking into a broad smile.

Again the room erupted, this time in laughter and applause. Duke and Henry embraced as everyone seemed to be talking at once. Henry is Duke's brother? He was there all the time to protect us?

"Oh no," quipped Kevin. "It's worse than Guervno. You're going to invite us back to Cortiza! But that is impossible. Are you still with IMM? We heard you were going to be fired if we

211

didn't succeed in six months."

"Slow down, everyone. I know I've got some explaining to do," Duke said, flashing his infectious boyish grin.

Everyone sat down, excited to hear what Duke had to say. "To tell you the truth, I thought my days at IMM were over. But worse yet, I was terrified that Ytefas and Henry would not be able to rescue you. I should have known that Henry would take care of you. He's not just the absent-minded professor he pretends to be. Thank God you're all back alive. That was all I cared about. Of course, as soon as the six-month deadline was up, Mr. J called a board meeting calling for my resignation and surrender of my stock options. Some day when we're all sitting around a camp-fire telling monster stories, I'll tell you about my friend Mr. J. Anyway, I was about to admit that Mr. J had finally won when my old friend Bill Mangle stood up and told me to sit down and shut up before I made a fool of myself. He took out a copy of the agreement and read one simple line: 'six months from the day the team members arrive at the El Frando Plant.' It took a second for those words to sink in. Then we all realized — you never made it to the plant. The six-month clock had never started.

"Mr. J just stood there, stunned. He took his cigar out of his mouth and suddenly screamed, 'Noooooo!' I was so startled, I nearly jumped out of my skin. Then he just turned around and left the room. He hasn't been back to the office since. The board fired him."

Henry stood up, "Duke, if you will give me a moment, I have some explaining to do, too. First, my dear friends, let me start by saying I am sorry for not sharing my identity with you. After my wife was killed, Duke asked me to go with him to Cortiza to visit the El Frando plant. It was there that I first met Ytefas. He had infiltrated Guervno's operations and kept the CIA apprised of his growing power. With the growing political unrest, the CIA asked that I stay, just to keep them informed on Guervno's movements. Let me stop here and say that none of us ever anticipated he would harm Americans — or those poor Canadians.

"Several days after your capture, Duke sent word to me that you were missing. One of my contacts in the jungle told me that Ytefas was your guard. He of course knew the way to our cabin and we prayed he could get you there safely. My operations are now declassified. Duke and I talked and decided it was time for us to share this with you. It is part of why you are here tonight."

Duke interrupted, "Enough about that, now let's get to Kevin's statement about me inviting you back to Cortiza. That's exactly what I'm going to do, my friends, and I hope every one of you will consider my offer. I need you. And I apologize sincerely for the ordeal you suffered — I feel responsible. You trusted me. And I put you in harm's way. Let's eat and have a glass of wine. I want to soften you up for my sales pitch. I'll answer all of your questions when we're done."

As the team began to eat, questions were swirling in their minds. They were served Caesar salad and shrimp cocktail, Beef Wellington and creme brulée. The conversation was animated and friends eagerly caught up on gossip. Nevertheless, throughout the meal, there was the tension of anticipation. What did Duke have in mind? More importantly, would anyone be willing to return to Cortiza? Was the El Frando plant still operational?

The conversation was interrupted as Duke stood up, clanging a spoon against his water glass. The lights in the room dimmed and a screen dropped silently from the ceiling. A video filled the screen. The first shots showed a jungle from the air fading to a shot of the Cortiza Airport. Several people whispered as they recognized the view. The camera zoomed in to a closeup, but the buildings looked transformed with a fresh coat of white paint. "Where are the guards?" Gary asked to no one in particular.

"Good question, Gary," answered Duke. "They're gone. The military no longer controls Cortiza. You may have been hearing about the civil war in Cortiza. It could have been bloody and brutal. Last month the capital fell. The rebels wanted to start a blood bath, but their new President has promised peace and order. He has already stopped the forced labor and given land back to the people."

"It *couldn't* be Guervno," Sharon remarked. "I can't imagine *him* promising peace!" Sharon shivered at the very memory of her captor. "I hope the new President can help that poor country," she added sincerely.

"No one has to worry about Guervno," said Duke smiling. "Guervno and his men have left the country. They had a short reign of terror in the countryside until Ytefas organized a resistance movement. Rumor has it that Guervno died of wounds, but even if he survived, his power is gone and most of his followers have scattered. Let's watch the rest of this short video. I think you'll be surprised."

The camera moved to the governmental headquarters. People walked freely in the marketplace. Everyone noted the lack of military guards. The camera entered the presidential palace and as the doors opened, they saw Ytefas! The five colleagues were astonished. Then the video abruptly stopped and the lights came on.

"Yes, my friends, Ytefas is acting President of Cortiza. He has called for national elections in 60 days. He has promised the people that there will be no more military governments. Cortiza will be a republic with an elected president and an elected National Congress, in accordance with the national constitution. Cortiza will have its first civilian government in 16 years. Ytefas will run for President, but there will be no more President for Life. The constitution of Cortiza states that the term of office is six years and that a President shall not serve a second term. It appears certain that Ytefas will win by a landslide. He is already a national hero and he has been able to keep bloodshed to a very minimum. He is preaching reconciliation and peace. And the United States has rushed to his aid with money to repair roads and schools and hospitals.

"Now I want to get back to my sales pitch. The El Frando plant is a mess. Of course, it was a mess nearly two years ago when you agreed to try to make that operation succeed. But our government is offering powerful incentives to American companies investing in this country. Powerful people in congress are welcoming another republic into the world community. Cortiza has a lot to offer: sugar, bananas, shrimp, petroleum, nickel, coffee. And our mine in El Frando has tremendous potential.

"This country is literally changing from week to week. Cable communications are being laid. The World Bank has extended a generous line of credit. Cortiza is actually purchasing millions of dollars of heavy machinery from America with the money. There are plans to build roads, even a permanent road to El Frando that won't collapse every monsoon season! There are no guarantees, of course, but there is a great deal of hope. There are so many valuable resources in Cortiza. With the right government, the people could begin improving their lives in just a few months. Ytefas has promised much higher wages for workers. He has so many dreams and plans, and I want to be a part of that.

"So here's my offer. I want you to go back to Cortiza. Ytefas has offered us a generous package of help from his government. No more bribes. No more visits from the military. This is a chance of a lifetime. Will you take another chance? There is really no reason why any of you should say 'yes.' It's still hot and rains all the time. The challenges are enormous. But I need you. You're the very best. And think of the adventure!"

Duke sat down to a silent room. After awkward seconds of silence, Kevin stood up.

"Eighteen months ago, I went to Cortiza to escape a failing marriage and three sons who hardly knew me. Now I'm committed to my wife. For the first time in my life, I'm actually in love. And I'm getting to know my three beautiful sons. But while you were talking, Duke, Susan squeezed my hand and whispered, 'Go.' I'm an engineer. And this is an engineer's chance of a lifetime. I'm in."

"Me too," said Gary, getting to his feet. "I'm taking my new svelte body back to that jungle and completing what I never really started."

One by one the others stood and joined in a circle. Duke watched in amazement, tears suddenly running down his cheeks.

"My friends, things are going to be a little different this time," promised Duke. "First of all, Ytefas has suggested that families join the engineering team. So, Kevin, you are welcome to invite your bride to join you in this venture. But if families want to stay home, you will alternate one month at El Frando and one month back in the States. It doesn't matter how long it takes, IMM is committed to making the operation work. Now I have something for each of you." Duke opened his briefcase and handed an envelope to each of the five. On the outside of each envelope was a TEF pin and the person's name. Inside was a contract, ready for signature, and a very large check. It was Duke's turn to laugh that deep, rich, resounding laugh that others found so irresistible.

"A toast to the next G-curve for Team El Frando," Michelle said as she raised her glass.

"A toast to each of you," Duke added.

The next adventure was about to begin.

Summit
Afterthoughts

Henry's Journal

I feel blessed that the team has come so far. Last night at our REUNION DINNER, I replayed in my mind everything each one of them had been through. The STORIES they had shared with me over the last EIGHTEEN MONTHS and the STRUGGLES they had each faced throughout their life time. Now each one of them has a entirely new idea of what a SIGNIFICANT emotional EXPERIENCE truly is. I'm EXCITED about what the future holds for them and their families. Each time a person finds the MISSING links, the balance, I still find wonder in the GROWTH they experience as a human being.

The next 18 MONTHS are going to be fasCINATING. If the team CAN continue to grow AND learn, and keep CLIMBing the spiralstaircase, then they will experience a WHOLE new level of LIVING. When they are READY, each one of them must find their passion. GARRETT is the only one who seems to understand the concept. One of the CHALLENGES will be HELPING them to uNDERSTAnd that simply ACHIEVING success in their field doesn't necessarily MEAN they have FOUND their passion. The fear of change will be THEIR greatest challenge.

MICHELLE sees herself as a computer specialist, the top in her field. If thAT TUrns out not to be her

PASSION, WILL SHE TAKE THE STEPS NECESSARY TO BREAK WITH THAT IDENTITY? It's SUCH A NECESSARY PART OF REACHING THE SUMMIT OF LIFE'S EXPERIENCE. ONE MUST SEARCH FOR THEIR PURPOSE. I HAVE WATCHED AND STUDIED SO MANY WHO BELIEVE THAT LIFE IS WHAT HAPPENS BEFORE EIGHT AND AFTER FIVE, NOT UNDERSTANDING THAT LIFE IS SO MUCH MORE. SO FEW EVER FIND THAT EXCEPTIONAL PLACE OF LIVING THAT I MUST PROVIDE ROLE MODELS FOR THEM TO STUDY. THE LIFE OF MAHATMA GANDHI, OF JOHN MARK TEMPLETON, THE IMPACT OF MOTHER THERESA AND MARTIN LUTHER KING EACH A GREAT EXAMPLE OF WHAT IT MEANS TO LIVE YOUR PURPOSE.

THE TEAM MUST GET OFF THE TREADMILL. WORKING HARDER IS NOT WHAT FINDING YOUR PASSION IS ABOUT. THEY MUST FIND WITHIN THEMSELVES THAT SPECIAL AND UNIQUE TALENT. AS EXAMPLES FOR MICHELLE, I WILL USE BUSINESS LEADERS WHOSE FOCUS ACCOMPLISHED INCREDIBLE RESULTS IN THE FIELD OF TECHNOLOGY.

GARY WOULD UNDERSTAND THE ZONE ATHLETES TALK ABOUT. THAT ULTIMATE EXPRESSION OF UNIQUE ABILITY THAT WE WATCHED HAPPEN WHEN MICHAEL JORDAN LEAPT FROM ALMOST MIDCOURT TO SCORE AND TIGER WOODS ACHIEVED AN UNPARALLELED VICTORY AT THE MASTERS. PASSION IS THAT UNIQUE GIFT THAT EVERY PERSON HAS, BUT VERY FEW FIND SIMPLY

BECAUSE THEY **NEVER** SEARCH! I MUST HELP THEM TO UNDERSTAND WHAT ZIG ZIGLAR MEANT WHEN HE SAID, "YOU WILL FIND YOUR PASSION WHEN YOU CATCH A GLIMPSE OF YOUR OWN POTENTIAL."

THE JUNGLE WAS GOOD FOR EVERYONE...INCLUDING ME. THE TIME OF SOLITUDE AND REFLECTION WERE VITAL TO MY ADJUSTING TO LIFE WITHOUT MY WIFE. THE DAILY PATH OF PRAYER, MEDITATION, REFLECTION, AND EXERCISE HAVE KEPT ME CENTERED THROUGH IT ALL. THE TEAM HAS BEEN AS MUCH A BLESSING TO ME, AS THEY SAY I AM TO THEM. I MUST CONTINUE TO LEARN. TO CLIMB THE UNENDING SPIRAL STAIRCASE. I MUST BE THE KIND OF PERSON OTHERS ARE ATTRACTED TO BECAUSE OF HOW I LIVE MY LIFE. KIDS NOW DESPERATELY WANT RESPECT, THEY CARRY GUNS AND MAKE THREATS. MEN AND WOMEN ARE SO BUSY CHASING THE ALMIGHTY DOLLAR THAT THEIR LIVES SHIFT OUT OF BALANCE. IF THEY COULD ONLY REALIZE THAT BOTH MONEY AND RESPECT ARE ATTRACTED. I MUST LIVE A LIFE WORTHY OF RESPECT AND WEALTH. MY PRIORITIES MUST STAY IN ORDER. I MUST CONTINUE TO BE A WHOLE PERSON WITHIN MYSELF, TO EXPERIENCE LIFE AT THE SUMMIT.

THE SECOND GCURVE OF TEAM EL FRANDO. WE'RE GOING BACK TO THE JUNGLE! DUKE CERTAINLY IS PASSIONATE ABOUT GETTING THAT PLANT UP AND RUNNING AND I AM LOOKING FORWARD TO SEEING

YTEFAS. I THINK EVEN THE TEAM WILL BE SURPRISED
BY THE LIFE CHANGES THAT CAN HAPPEN THIS NEXT 18
MONTHS. I AM PROUD OF DUKE FOR ACKNOWLEDGING
THE NEED FOR THE TEAM TO SPEND TIME WITH THEIR
ENCOURAGE FAMILIES. HE IS DEVELOPING AN UNDERSTANDING OF
HIM TO   PRIORITIES. I CAN SEE HIS SELF CONCEPT DUKE-FIND
FIND   SOMEONE TO
RELATIONSHIPS IMPROVING. MAYBE ONE DAY HE CAN COME TO   MENTOR
ROMANCE
          UNDERSTAND OUR FATHER AND LET GO OF
THAT MANSION WE GREW UP IN. I GUESS I WILL
KNOW WHEN I HEAR IMM IS LOOKING FOR A NEW
RETREAT HOUSE.

Dr. Tom Hill
Background

Dr. Tom Hill is the CEO of The Goal Coach Companies™LLC headquartered in Lake St. Louis, Missouri. In addition to authoring *Living At The Summit: A Novel Approach to an Exceptional Life,* Tom is also the co-author of the soon-to-be-published *Chicken Soup for the Entrepreneurial Soul,* which is scheduled for release in 1999.

Divisions of The Goal Coach Companies include The Eagle Institute, an organization devoted solely to assisting others find and follow their life's passion and Goal Coach Publishing which publishes a variety of personal development products. A unique component of The Eagle Institute is its Youth Division which provides personal development training and mentoring to young people ages 13-21.

Dr. Hill is a renowned speaker, workshop leader and teacher. He offers a variety of compelling topics delivered as a keynote speech, a workshop or seminar. He has spoken to thousands nationwide, including the Young President's Organization, RE/MAX and community organizations throughout the country.

In 1986, after more than two decades in education, Dr. Hill changed careers and embarked on a path which was to take him to a level of success he had only dreamed of. Cashing in his state retirement plan and selling his home, he launched a new business, building it into a $3 billion enterprise in less than 10 years. Dr. Hill realized that his story would serve as inspiration to others. He is a living example that it is never to late to follow your heart's desire. Today, Dr. Hill has returned to teaching, sharing his special gifts with individuals and audiences nationwide through the divisions of The Goal Coach Companies.

Dr. Hill served as Superintendent of Schools - Missouri Public Schools from 1964-1971. From 1972 through 1986 he served as a member of the faculty and as administrator for the University of Missouri - Columbia. He received his BS in Social Science from the University of Missouri - Columbia in 1960, his Masters in Education Administration in 1963 from Northeast Missouri State University and his Doctorate in Administration and Adult Education from the University of Missouri - Columbia in 1975.

Dr. Hill and his wife, Betty, have 6 children and 7 grandchildren. They make their home in Lake St. Louis, Missouri.

John P. Gardner, Jr.
Background

John Gardner is the President of The Goal Coach Companies™ LLC which is headquartered in Lake St. Louis, Missouri. In addition to co-authoring *Living At The Summit: A Novel Approach to an Exceptional Life*, he is also the co-author of *Chicken Soup for the Entrepreneurial Soul* which is scheduled for release in 1999.

A compelling speaker and presenter, Mr. Gardner delivers his thought-provoking programs to audiences nationwide. His combination of unique insights on the impact of technology and future trends that will continue to shape our world in the new millennium, keeps his audiences' rapt attention. A lifelong student, Mr. Gardner continues his personal education, always searching for answers, new challenges and information on a daily basis. He believes personal passion is the key to exceptional living.

With his business partner, Dr. Tom Hill, he has founded The Eagle Institute, an organization dedicated to providing individuals with personal development tools, resources and access to leadership through a variety of programs. Mr. Gardner is committed to helping others achieve success. The epitome of servant leadership, he believes his true calling lies in serving as a role model and mentor for others.

Prior to his involvement with The Goal Coach Companies, Mr. Gardner spent more than twenty years as an attorney, building one of the largest legal practices in South Carolina. He served eight years in the South Carolina General Assembly and was elected by his peers to the Department of Highways and Public Transportation Commission.

Mr. Gardner received both his undergraduate and law degree in only five and one-half years. He graduated second in his class from Wofford College in Spartanburg, South Carolina and received his Juris Doctor from the University of South Carolina - School of Law at age 22.

An active volunteer, he currently serves on the Coker College Board of Visitors. Active at the local and regional level, Mr. Gardner has held a variety of positions, including Chairman of the Darlington County Development Board.

Mr. Gardner, and his wife Elizabeth, have four children and are lifelong residents of Darlington, South Carolina.

Elizabeth Gardner

Elizabeth Gardner is a talented writer, professional speaker and trainer who has inspired thousands of people nationwide with her message of personal and professional potential. Over the past 5 years, she has delivered workshops and training programs on balancing family life with a career, effective team management and communication skills.

Elizabeth, along with her husband John, and their business partner Dr. Tom Hill, are co-founders of The Eagle Institute, an organization dedicated to helping others find their life's passion and fulfill their potential. Elizabeth is committed to helping others, particularly women, learn the techniques and skills that have helped her to continue to achieve her life's dreams.

She began her career as an award winning interior designer with a firm in South Carolina, and is the former Director of Marketing for The Gardner Law Firm. In that capacity, she was responsible for the firm's 1994 award from the American Bar Association for the most dignified advertising campaign for a law firm in the nation. Elizabeth attended Columbia College in Columbia, South Carolina, where she majored in interior design. She furthered her studies in England where she studied with the Interior Design Society. In addition, she majored in marketing and business administration at Coker College in Hartsville, South Carolina.

The Gardners are the parents of four children, ranging in age from pre-school to young adult. They are committed to serving as role models for their children in terms of life balance and priorities. They are lifelong residents of Darlington, South Carolina.

Recommended
Reading

The following list of materials has been compiled for your convenience. It contains all of the publications/ tapes recommended within Living At The Summit.

Barnhart, Tod. (1995).
The Five Rituals of Wealth. New York: Harper Collins.

Benson, M.D., Herbert and Klipper, Miriam Z. (1990).
The Relaxation Response. Avon.

Branden, Nathaniel. (1995).
The Six Pillars of Self-Esteem. New York: Bantam Books.

Canfield, Jack and Hansen, Mark Victor. (1995).
The Aladdin Factor: How to Ask for and Get Everything You Want. New York: Berkley Publishing Group.

Canfield, Jack. (1989).
How to Build High Self-Esteem. Chicago, IL: Nightingale-Conant

Chilton, David. (1998).
The Wealthy Barber. Updated Third Edition. Prima Publishing.

Cooper, M.D., Kenneth. (1998).
Advanced Nutritional Therapies. Thomas Nelson.

Foster, Richard. (1998)
Celebration of Discipline: The Path to Spiritual Growth. Harper.

Fromm, Erich. (1989).
The Art of Loving. Reissue Edition. Harper-Collins.

Gray, John. (1992).
Men Are From Mars, Women Are from Venus: A Practical Guide for Improving Communication and Getting What You Want in Your Relationships. Harper-Collins.

Hansen, Mark Victor and Canfield, Jack. (1996).
Dare to Win. New York: BerkleyPublishing Group.

Hardcastle, Bob. (1994).
Money Talk: Simple Secrets for Financial Security. AMACOM.

Harris, Blaine and Coonradt, Charles. (1996).
Four Laws of Debt-Free Prosperity. Chequemate International, Inc.

Herrmann, Ned. (1996).
The Whole Brain Business Book. New York: McGraw-Hill Book Company.

Hill, Napoleon. (1990).
Think & Grow Rich. Reissue Edition. Fawcett Books.

Jaworski, Joseph and Flowers, Betty. (1998).
Synchronicity: The Inner Path to Leadership. Barrett-Koehler.

Maltz, Maxwell. (1987).
Psycho-Cybernetics. Pocket Books.

Rand, Ayn. (1996).
Atlas Shrugged. Reissue Edition. Signet

Rogers, Jim. (1995).
Investment Biker: On the Road with Jim Rogers. Adams Publishing.

Rohn, Jim.
Challenge to Succeed in the 90's: A Philosophy for Successful Living.
Jim Rohn International. (800-929-0434).

Smalley, Gary. (1997).
Making Love Last Forever. Ward Books

Tracy, Brian. (1984).
Psychology of Achievement. Chicago, IL: Nightingale-Conant

Winfrey, Oprah and Greene, Bob. (1996).
Make the Connection: Ten Steps to a Better Body and a Better Life.
Hyperian Books.

Zukav, Gary. (1994).
Dancing Wu Li Masters: An Overview of the New Physics. Reissue
Edition. Bantam Books.

The Eagle Institute

Introduction

The concepts in this book are the result of many years of study and implementation in the lives of the co-authors. The principles set forth in *Living At The Summit* have been brought to life within a company, appropriately named The Eagle Institute. Dr. Tom Hill and John and Elizabeth Gardner created The Institute after realizing that the keys to reaching the summit of life experience were having the necessary information for continuing growth, coupled with the access to, and the influence of, those few people already living an exceptional life.

The Eagle Institute is a company created for those individuals who are already successful. They have proven their desire to achieve, their tenacity, and their commitment to excel. But somehow life still remains a different picture than the one they were striving to create. The balance, freedom, and passion of daily life are still an illusion.

There are several components that create the Eagle Membership Advantage. At quarterly events, members will meet with some of the world's most exceptional individuals; sharing ideas and resources for the benefit of each member. In addition, monthly packages of information will be sent to the membership to create the foundation for a growing Library for Exceptional Living tailored to the five key areas of life. To maximize today's technology, members will receive The Eagle Institute's e-zine. It will consistently provide insights from CEOs, successful entrepreneurs, investment experts, health professionals, relationship experts, and spiritual leaders. It is the ultimate electronic magazine with cutting edge ideas for living a truly exceptional life.

If you are interested in more information on The Eagle Institute, please visit our web site at www.eagleinstitute.com. For anyone who would like to receive an application, please call us at 888-850-8761.

Living *at the* SUMMIT

Contact Information

Please visit our website

www.eagleinstitute.com

Or contact our authors

Tom Hill ... thill@eagleinstitute.com

John Gardner... jpgjr@eagleinstitute.com

Elizabeth Gardner... egardner@eagleinstitute.com

1325 Lake St. Louis Boulevard, Suite 150
Lake St. Louis, Missouri 63367

Order Form

For additional copies of *Living At The Summit*, please complete and send the following:

A Novel Approach to an Exceptional Life

SHIPPING INFORMATION

NAME

ADDRESS

CITY   STATE   ZIP

DAYTIME PHONE

SEND TO
GOAL COACH PUBLISHING
1325 LAKE ST. LOUIS BOULEVARD
SUITE 150
LAKE ST. LOUIS, MISSOURI 63367

FOR OFFICE USE ONLY
DATE
FILLED
SHIPPED

CALL 1-888-850-8761 OR FAX 314-625-2145

DR. TOM HILL

WITH JOHN & ELIZABETH GARDNER

PAYMENT INFORMATION

- ☐ CHECK NO.
- ☐ VISA   ☐ MASTERCARD
- ☐ DISCOVER   ☐ AMERICAN EXPRESS

☐☐☐☐☐☐☐☐☐☐☐☐☐☐☐☐

EXPIRES _____ / _____

SIGNATURE

Goal Coach Publishing

	No. of Copies	TOTAL
SOFT COVER **$11.95**		
SIGNED HARDCOVER **$24.95**		
SHIPPING/HANDLING $4.50 (1) .50 each additional copy		
TOTAL ENCLOSED		

Additional
Products

Please contact us for information regarding purchase of the following products. Prices do not include shipping & handling.

HARDCOVER LIMITED EDITION
Living At The Summit:
A Novel Approach to an Exceptional Life
A unique gift, each numbered copy is signed by the authors.

$24.95

SUGGESTED LISTENING FOR FURTHER
HELPFUL INSIGHTS
- Goal Setting for the 21st Century: The New Rules
By Dr. Tom Hill, John P. Gardner, Jr., Kerry Avant & Richard F. Baker, Jr. Learn simple yet extremely powerful concepts that shatter everything you thought you knew about goal setting. Understand the principles behind and beyond global networking for prosperity. Enter the 21st Century prepared.

$59.95

- The Eagle's Path for Entrepreneurs
By Dr. Tom Hill, John P. Gardner, Jr., and Rodney Sommerville
Discover the fast track to success. Learn the secrets that can propel your business to extraordinary levels. Uncover the keys to your amazing potential.

$59.95

SPECIAL TOOLS TO TRACK YOUR PROGRESS
- Eagle Journal   By Rebecca McDannold and Kathy Baker
Unique among journals, the Eagle Journal includes special sections for recording your dreams and aspirations for each area of life. A companion to Living At The Summit, this journal will become the cornerstone of your journey along the Eagle's path.

$19.95

- The Eagle Institute Journal
Printed exclusively for The Eagle Institute, this black leather-bound journal includes 128 gilt-edge pages for recording your goals, insights and progress. The Eagle Institute name is embossed on the cover in gold.

$24.95